PLAYS TWO

Martin Crimp was born in 1956. His plays include *Definitely the Bahamas* (1987), *Dealing with Clair* (1988), *Play with Repeats* (1989), *No One Sees the Video* (1990), *Getting Attention* (1991), *The Treatment* (winner of the 1993 John Whiting Award), *Attempts on Her Life* (1997), *The Country* (2000), *Face to the Wall* (2002) and *Cruel and Tender* (2004). A short fiction, *Stage Kiss,* was published in 1991 and *Four Imaginary Characters* appeared in 2000 as a preface to *Plays One*. In 2004 the French and German premieres of the short play *Fewer Emergencies* were staged at the Théâtre National de Chaillot and the Schaubühne in Berlin. He has also translated works by Ionesco, Koltès, Genet, Marivaux and Molière.

by the same author

MARTIN CRIMP PLAYS ONE
(*Dealing with Clair, Play with Repeats,*
Getting Attention, The Treatment)

THREE ATTEMPTED ACTS
(in *Best Radio Plays of 1985*)

FACE TO THE WALL and FEWER EMERGENCIES

CRUEL AND TENDER

Translations

THE CHAIRS (Ionesco)
ROBERTO ZUCCO (Koltès)
THE MAIDS (Genet)
THE TRIUMPH OF LOVE (Marivaux)
THE FALSE SERVANT (Marivaux)

MARTIN CRIMP

Plays Two

No One Sees the Video

The Misanthrope

Attempts on Her Life

The Country

Introduced
by the author

ff

faber and faber

This collection first published in 2005
by Faber and Faber Limited
3 Queen Square London WC1N 3AU

Typeset by Country Setting, Kingsdown, Kent CT14 8ES
Printed in England by Mackays of Chatham plc, Chatham, Kent

2 4 6 8 10 9 7 5 3

Contents

Four Unwelcome Thoughts

WHEN THE ACTOR PULLS OUT

When the actor pulls out, he wants the writer to be assured it's nothing to do with the script, or the personality of the director, who is sitting in the back of the car, smiling angrily. No no no, his reasons are personal, his life's complicated, he made a commitment – yes yes – obviously – but things have changed since then, he's a human being and his decisions must be respected. The theatre makes demands – of course – no one's denying that – but so does life, so does life.

The car is stuck in traffic. The red brake-lights ahead of them glow constantly in an unbroken line all the way from here to the intersecting boulevard. Shoppers criss-cross the street right in front of them with their bags of cheese, whole crabs, sticks of bread. Already late. And now this ridiculous phone call. Even the driver, a man who drives every day, whose job it is to drive, to endure traffic – even the driver seems angry. Look at the way he bangs the pads of his hands against the steering-wheel, as if, by doing this, he could push the car forwards.

The writer feels sick. 'Nothing to do with the script'? He finds that hard to believe. If it's nothing to do with the script, why did the actor feel the need to mention it? He begins to play the actor's lines in his head: every word crumbles. He needs to call the actor back and be re-assured. But how can he degrade himself by calling the actor back? The director has already done everything possible. And besides (the director warns him) the actor has made it quite clear through his intermediaries that there is nothing more to discuss. What d'you mean, says the writer, 'through his intermediaries'? Truth dawns: the actor won't even speak to them.

The writer works his way back into the play. He pushes open the doors, turns on the taps, tries the switches. He pulls up the floorboards and examines the wiring. He puts his ear to the plaster and listens: he can hear it drying, and as it dries he can hear it crack. He starts hacking the plaster off the walls so he can see the naked brick. The naked brick appals him. Everything he's made is shoddy and incomplete. The bricks are split. Nothing works. There are light switches, yes, and bulbs hanging from the ceiling, but where are the wires connecting them? It's all a sham. The whole building should be condemned! His bowels ache. He shits in the toilet, but even the toilet is faulty: however many times he flushes it, that shit, that secret stinking part of himself, remains floating in the shit-stained water where everyone can see it. And even his most precious word, the word he placed so carefully on the toilet floor before undoing his trousers, even that precious word suddenly extends its legs and before he can catch it – hey! – scuttles into a crack.

The car moves one car-length forward, bringing it level with a café. Here are the cups of coffee, here are the glasses of wine and beer, here on the pavement tables are the sandwiches and ashtrays that make life worth living. The customers lean back in their chairs to enjoy the October dusk, not simply indifferent to the traffic, but relishing its slow parade.

I FELT SO STUPID

I felt so stupid, the writer said to me, about the man with no arms. He was making his way towards me along the train, and everything about him – the cheap clothes, the strapped-on money-belt, and most of all the exposed stumps of unequal length – everything about him made it clear to me the man was begging. To expose those stumps of his seemed particularly cynical, given that the stumps were quite long, long enough to be fitted with prosthetic arms, something that even a poor man would be entitled to, surely. No no, it was clear to me he'd left his artificial arms at home quite deliberately, so that the naked stumps would make maximum impact.

So you can imagine how ashamed I felt (the writer went on) when the man simply found an empty seat and sat in it. He wasn't begging at all, he was simply, like myself, an 'ordinary' passenger – even if – and of course this did confuse me – even if he happened to be wearing the money-belt which I had assumed meant begging. This money belt, you see, had a zip. Now I could just about imagine a situation where a beggar invited you to open the zip, put in your money, and close the zip again. But given that the man was not a beggar – d'you see what I'm saying? – given that he was an ordinary passenger, how could he possibly use, all on his own, a man with no hands, a zip-up money-belt?

I couldn't answer that question, and wasn't sure why the writer was telling me this. Don't people make these small embarrassing mistakes every day? – misjudgements, might be a better word – and are they really so worth talking about? If he was trying to be intimate with me – and of course people often do reveal weaknesses in an attempt to force intimacy – then he was going about it the wrong way. Weakness of any kind disgusts me. And besides, it's always a mistake to sleep with a client – particularly one who so obviously dyes his hair.

I asked the waiter for the bill and, when I'd paid it and got back the change, reached behind me for my jacket. But the writer stopped me. There was one more thing he wanted to tell me about the man with no arms – something – he smiled when he said this – something that made him even more ashamed. And that was the fear he had, as the man with no arms came down the train towards him, exactly like a beggar (as he then thought) 'working' the train, the fear that this man would pick his pockets.

Pick your pockets? I said.

Yes, he admitted – smiling even more, and trying to stand one of the small coins I'd left on the table up on its edge – as he came closer I'm ashamed to say I wrapped my coat more tightly around me so he wouldn't be able to reach into my pockets and steal my money or my mobile telephone.

THE DIRECTORS ARE SQUEEZED

The directors are squeezed into the bottom left-hand corner of a huge black square of paint. The explanatory text says 'this conveys the tension of the theatre' – but isn't this black mass surrounding three human heads more a device to mask the picture's and therefore the painter's insignificance?

The writer is very pleased with himself when he thinks of this. He begins to make a mental list of what is now impossible: the painted portrait (obviously), the well-made play (hilarious), the radical (oh really?) gesture, political engagement (ha ha ha!). The more examples of impossibility and failure he comes up with, the happier he is. The more bloodshed, the more death (he was right all along about that war, by the way), the more chaos, the more terror. The more bad faith, the more bad sex, the more bad art. Wonderful! And now to top it all this so-called 'portrait' of directors tipped out of their comfy theatre into the corner of a black square. It can only confirm his very worst fears – which is all he has ever asked out of life.

WHEN THE WRITER KILLS HIMSELF

When the writer kills himself, the other writers feel like they've been punched – just here – in the stomach. They're up on the marble roof of a cathedral – in Milan, as it happens – and when they hear the news they stagger towards the edge and only just save themselves from toppling off. So. The writer has killed himself! What a terrible thing! It's like being punched – just here – in the stomach! They gaze up at the stone saints on their pinnacles. The clear blue sky starts spinning.

When the sick feeling has gone, the writers make their way back down the spiral stairs and head straight for their bookshelves. They pull out the works of the writer who killed himself and examine them for clues. The texts are short and few in number – after all, the writer was very young, so the body of work is small. And it's not long before they find evidence: a word here, an image there (the hot ash, for example, falling onto the child's eyeball), and of course the self-lacerating dialogue. Hold the pages up to the light and it's like a watermark or a security-feature in a banknote: each sheet of paper turns out to be indelibly marked 'suicide'. Why did no one notice this? Why was no action taken?

The writers put on black and join the cortège. The coffin ahead of them glows slightly, filled, as it is, with the dense isotope of genius. When the earth is shovelled in, each writer sees it fall from the coffin's point of view because of those films they've watched where a camera is installed at the bottom of a grave, pointing upwards through a sheet of glass. As the screen goes black, they shudder.

The writers leave Milan.

When asked how they feel, what else can they do but smile and shake their heads?

When asked to give interviews, it is only with extreme reluctance that they accept.

When asked to explain the significance of the work, they rub their eyes with their knuckles as they patiently reply that its significance lies precisely in its resistance to explanatory discourse.

When the retrospectives begin, when the work of the writer who killed himself is restaged and reassessed, the writers who are left offer their full support: they sit in the front row, they concentrate on every phrase, they climb into the structure of the writing as only writers can, not afraid to be cut – and they often are – on the sharp edges. They look round fiercely at the critics, daring them not to perceive the work's truth and beauty. But for once the critics have understood. In bed on a Sunday morning the writers drink in their dead young colleague's long and reverential reviews

At night, though, things are different. The writers find themselves waking up in the dark with an unpleasant feeling in their mouths: they've been grinding their teeth. All this homage, all this reverence: the dead writer is getting on their nerves. This monstrous self-promotion! Not only did he make sense of his life by ending it, but he made sense of his work too, quite deliberately. There the work is – complete, finite – while the rest of us (they think) are forced to go on struggling for recognition, never knowing whether what we produce will consolidate our reputation or – far more likely, given those idiot critics – undermine it. How sensible to die! Especially in the theatre! The writers look at the clock. Only 2 a.m. They go into the bathroom and turn on the light. They notice with loathing the hairs growing round their nipples, some of which – ugh – are already grey. When they yawn, the gold caps on their decaying molars glint back at them. We too (they think) would like to die – only we're too old, and have too many responsibilities.

When they finally get back to sleep the phone rings: please would you write an introduction to the dead writer's complete works? They are all too weary to refuse.

The nasty taste of tooth-grinding won't go away: Paris, London, Vienna, Berlin, wherever the remaining writers go, the dead one is filling theatres and making the universities hum. They fly to Milan. They climb back onto the roof of the cathedral. But even here, even among the stone saints, the hum is audible. They insert soft plastic ear-plugs. They realise it is their own brains humming.

The following Wednesday the theatre invites the writers to lunch. It's a serve-yourself affair, but there's a big choice of vegetables, salads, and meat. More importantly perhaps, the long white table has plenty of wine on it. In theory the writers are angry – what's this lunch all about, anyway? – please not another commemoration – but already the sight of those bottles on the long white table helps to appease them. They pile their plates with chicken and vegetables, salads and fish, sit down and reach out for the wine. The director waits till the glasses are full, then makes a short speech. Despite our loss, he says, or perhaps, he adds, because of it, I believe the moment has now come, he says, to look to the future, to affirm that all of you gathered round this table, he says, each with your own distinctive voice and talent, he says, are not just the intelligence, if I can put it that way, but also the life-blood of this theatre. He proposes a toast and all the writers drink – yes! – to the future, taking care to meet each others' eyes. And each one at that moment has the same insight, and the same secret thought, and each one knows that only he is the one to have had this secret secret thought, which is: *the future means me*. Yes, it was that strange meeting of eyes that made each one see – 'in a flash' – the mediocrity of all the others. And with that came the revelation: *there is no longer any competition*. Now that the dead writer is dead, now that there's no longer the threat of genius, now that even genius itself has been tested, approved and filed away, *the field is clear.*

We writers feel fresher and more alive than we have for months. We clap our hands. We pour out another glass of wine – even if the white is by now unpleasantly warm. Each of us looks at the fool opposite, and wonders what that smile means.

MC, October 2004

NO ONE SEES THE VIDEO

A viable culture consists of ways of evading the questions, of inhibiting an insistent inquiry into them, for there are no answers.

Ernest Gellner
Recollection in Anxiety

Author's Note

Between 1980 and 1983 I worked intermittently for various Market Research companies, transcribing audio-tapes of groups and depths.

A *depth* is an intensive one-to-one interview. A *group* is a discussion involving six to eight people. The purpose of groups and depths is often to introduce people to *concepts,* which are ideas for commercials. (*Group* may also mean classification by age/sex/social class.) To *probe* is to elicit a response. To *prompt* is to suggest or anticipate a response.

No One Sees the Video was first performed at the Royal Court Theatre Upstairs, London, on 22 November 1990. The cast was as follows:

Karen/Sally Adie Allen
John/Roger/Nigel Michael Attwell
Colin Neil Dudgeon
Liz Celia Imrie
Jo Emer McCourt
Paul Stephen Tompkinson

Directed by Lindsay Posner
Designed by Simon Vincenzi
Lighting by Steve Whitson
Music by Graeme Miller

Time

Act One: March
Act Two: April
Act Three: April of the following year

Place

All locations are in the South West of London,
except for the Feathers Hotel which is in
the North East of England

Characters

South West London

Elizabeth
thirty-five

Karen
twenty-three

Colin
thirty-two

John
forty-four

Joanna
fifteen

Sally
seventeen

Roger
forty

North East England

Nigel
forty-four

Paul
twenty-three

Karen and Sally are played by the same actress.
John, Roger and Nigel are played by the same actor

Notes on the Text

An oblique stroke (/) indicates the exact point of interruption in overlapping dialogue.

Brackets ( ) indicate momentary changes of tone (usually a drop in projection).

A comma on a separate line

,

replaces 'Pause', 'Slight Pause' and the rest of it. The exact duration of any hiatus may be inferred from the context.

Act One

I.I STREET

Liz and Karen.

Karen Excuse me. Excuse me, Madam.

Liz Sorry?

Karen Yes, I wonder if I could ask you a few questions?

Liz Questions. What kind of / questions?

Karen Just about shopping.

Liz This isn't a good time. I'm sorry.

Karen Just a minute of your time.

Liz I'm sorry.

Karen Just a minute of your time, that's all.

Liz A minute.

Karen Really. Yes. One minute. Please.

,

Liz OK.

Karen OK?

Liz Well OK.

,

Karen Thank you. Right. Do you ever . . .?

Liz If I could just put down this bag . . .

Karen Fine, that's fine.

9

Liz What's this actually about?

Karen Shopping. It's about . . . well it's about shopping. Can you tell me if you ever use any of the following products nowadays?

Liz (Shopping.)

Karen Frozen pizzas.

Liz Sorry?

Karen Do you ever use frozen pizzas nowadays?

Liz Use them?

Karen Yes, I mean buy, eat, buy for your family, use.

Liz Yes.

Karen You do.

Liz Yes.

Karen Would you say that was often, frequently, occasionally or rarely?

Liz (What?) No, I'm sorry, would you / repeat that.

Karen Certainly. Often, frequently / occasionally . . .

Liz Yes, quite frequently.

Karen Frequently. Fine. Do you use other frozen pre-cooked Italian dishes nowadays?

Liz I'm sorry?

Karen Do you ever use other frozen pre-cooked Italian dishes?

Liz No.

Karen Fine. Is that no never or no rarely? (I'm talking about these are products such as lasagne / canelloni . . .)

Liz I'm sorry, but what is this in fact about?

Karen Shopping. Is that never or just rarely?

Liz (I don't know.)

Karen Well I'll put rarely.

Liz Listen.

Karen Yes?

Liz Listen.

Karen Of course.

Liz Can we stop this?

Karen We've nearly finished.

Liz I'd like to stop.

Karen D'you want to see my ID?

Liz It's not that, it's the subject.

Karen Italian meals.

Liz I mean the subject.

Karen This is my card. (The subject?) Look: this is me. I'm Karen. And that's the company I work for. OK?

,

I shouldn't tell you this but I'm going to tell you this: I get paid (it's quite simple) I get paid by the number of people who respond.

Liz I see. (So by respond, you mean . . .)

Karen This is a legitimate company. I'm just working for them.

Liz I see that.

Karen But what I can do is is I can fill in most of this later if you like.

Liz I'd rather you didn't do that.

Karen Because I'm quite happy to do that.

Liz I'd like to stop.

Karen I'm happy to do that but if you could just tell me are you married, single or separated stroke divorced?

Liz No. I'm sorry. My daughter is waiting for me.

Karen Good. May I assume then that you're married?

Liz No. Well yes. Obviously. In a sense.

Karen That's fine. Is that separated?

Liz No. Look.

Karen Because I'm happy to make up the rest but I'm not happy to make up marital status.

Liz My husband . . . Listen.

,

He seems . . . Well I mean he *has* . . . This morning, in the night . . . (What does it matter, the time of day?)

,

He's . . . (I mean gone.) He's left me.

,

He didn't come home last night, and this morning (Why am I telling you this?) there was, all there was, what he left, he'd left, in fact this is what he did, he left a message on the machine.

,

Karen This is an answering machine.

Liz A message on the answering machine.

Karen That's terrible. What shall I put?

'

No, I understand, because I really hate those machines.
What would you like me to put?

Liz I really don't care.

Karen I understand. Look, I'm putting you down as
married. I shouldn't do that but I'll do that so that you
qualify.

Liz How d'you mean: qualify?

Karen Can you tell me your husband's profession?

Liz What d'you mean: qualify?

Karen To take part in a depth interview. I'm sorry, but
I really do need husband's profession.

Liz (Writer, he's a writer.)

Karen A writer. OK. What this involves – no, that's
fascinating, is he famous? – what it involves is a one-
hour interview with one of our executives on Wednesday
the fourteenth (which is i.e. a week from now) at 8.30
p.m. in the Masonic Hall and for your participation you
will receive a small cash gift.

Liz Uh-huh.

'

Listen.

Karen Writer. That's fascinating. I don't have a
classification for that. Let's say upper managerial. That
makes him an A. If he's an A, you're an A.

'

Look, I can see you have views about this.

Liz That's exactly right.

Karen And that's good. That's exactly what they'll want. They'll want your views.

Liz Because I feel very strongly.

Karen That's good. That's what they'll want.

Liz Because I feel very strongly and I resent, I have to say that I resent the assumption that I will do something I have no desire to do, for payment.

Karen There's no payment, there's only the gift.

Liz Then what is the gift?

Karen How much is the gift?

Liz No. What is the gift?

Karen 'What is the gift?' D'you mean how much? (Because offhand . . .)

Liz I mean 'What?'

Karen It's not a thing. It's money.

Liz That's what I'm saying.

Karen It's not a thing. It's not some useless (I don't know) wristwatch. OK? It's not a voucher that has to be redeemed.

'

It's a gift of money, that's all it is.

Liz I'm sorry.

Karen So you're just going to walk away.

Liz I'm sorry.

Karen There's no obligation to accept the gift.

Liz (It's not the gift.)

Karen (Although most people obviously do.)

Liz I'm not talking about the gift.

Karen Then what are you talking about? Are you saying you won't participate?

Liz I'm saying I'd rather not participate.

Karen OK.

,

Perhaps I'd rather not do this. Perhaps I'd rather not be standing here in the street.

Both faint laugh.

OK?

Liz I'm sorry.

Karen Don't worry. One more thing. Do you work?

Liz Work. No.

Karen Do you have in that case (if I could just ask) if you have in that case any other source of income?

Blackout.

1.2 PUB

Colin and John.

Colin I'll tell you something: no one is going to tell me what to think.

John Well I admire that.

Colin Not a newspaper. (Thank you.) Not a television. Not a religion. No one. Take events in Europe. Have you seen those events in Europe?

John You mean the Wall.

Colin The Wall.

John The free elections.

Colin Elections, revolutions, I mean all of that.

John Because I think there's been too much of it.

Colin Too true there's been too much of it, but I'll tell you what I'm getting at, because what I'm getting at is, is no one is going to tell me what to think about those events. Because I pick up a paper – alright? – and I read about a new dawn . . .

John A new dawn . . .

Colin I read about a new dawn for Europe. But then I pick up something else and what's it about? It's about unrest, ethnic violence, disintegration. And what I'm saying is, is I don't want to be told, I want to decide.

,

John So what's your opinion of –

Colin I don't have an opinion.

John Uh-huh. (Meaning that . . .)

Colin I don't have an opinion and what I'm saying is, is that is my right.

John I admire that.

Colin They can fuck themselves. (Thank you.) People who have a playwright running the country, these must be people whose mission in life it is to suffer.

John Well it makes you weep.

Colin It makes you weep because they have brought that *upon* themselves. Which is of course their democratically elected right to do that.

John It's freedom of choice.

Colin (Exactly.) It's what?

John It's freedom of choice.

Colin Exactly.

,

Choice. Exactly. Because no one's going to tell me that I'm made of these things and that because of these *things*, these *acids*, I am in some way programmed to behave . . .

John (It's an insult.)

Colin (That's right. To our dignity.) . . . to behave in a particular way. I mean who *are* these people?

John It's cultural.

Colin (Of course it is.) It's what?

John It's cultural.

Colin Of course it is.

John And that's why you can learn about Moslems, you can learn about homosexuals, but the fact remains that to me these things are a mental illness.

Colin Uh-huh.

,

Well I take your point, but I have to say that individually –

John Individually, yes, they can be contained. We have minorities working for us, and they are as reasonable as you or me. In fact we have a policy . . .

Colin On their own.

John Yes, on their own, taken / on their own.

Colin We're recruiting minorities.

John So then you know. But take them in a mass . . .

Colin A mass is something else . . .

John When you see them in a stadium and their fists are clenched . . .

Colin Well you're talking about power . . .

John Or they're screaming for somebody's *death*.

,

Colin I'll tell you what I resent and that's when I'm told I should not have sex.

John What, this is some kind of medical / advice?

Colin I'm talking about / the dreaded.

John My brother-in-law had an infarct and he was advised / not to.

Colin No, I'm talking about the dreaded. Because I get some leaflet about the dreaded and what's the gist of it? The gist of it is, is thou shalt not. OK, so it's safe to masturbate with my partner, but let's face it I don't need a partner to do that.

John Surely.

Colin And before you know where you are like everything else it's twisted into some kind of moral issue: stay within marriage, one faithful partner. Because why should I be *limited* in that way?

,

18

John I am a married man as a matter of fact.

Colin I respect that. Don't think I don't respect that. But if I happen to see maybe this part of the leg – I'm sorry, I don't know your name –

John John.

Colin If I happen to see, John, this part of the leg, or maybe it's the hairs, those little soft hairs at the back of the neck.

John I know what / you mean.

Colin D'you know what I mean?

,

And for all I know this could be a young, a very young girl.

John A minor.

Colin Well perhaps technically . . .

,

Don't misunderstand me, John. OK – it's lunchtime – I like a drink at lunchtime – and like yourself, I'm just opening my heart.

John I have a girl and a boy.

Colin I think that's wonderful. One of each. A lucky man.

John My daughter is fourteen.

Colin Is that right?

,

Is that right? Because don't for godsake mis / understand me.

John Chris is fourteen, but some of her friends, some of Chris's friends that she brings home, they look a lot older.

Colin Well of course they do.

,

Of course they do, and that's human.

John It worries me. I'll be honest.

Colin Don't let it worry you.

John Because I think it's wrong, the way they dress.

Colin Don't let it worry you.

John You think it's human?

Colin I *know* it's human. The leg, the little hairs, there will be a response to that, which is human. OK, you can say 'this is right,' 'this is wrong,' but you cannot stop the response.

John Which is why we have laws.

Colin We have laws. (You're quite right.) And what do the laws do? The laws testify to the strength of these feelings. I like that kind of name.

John What kind of name is that?

Colin When a girl has a boy's name. Chris.

John I'd never thought / of that.

Colin Hadn't you thought of that? Because I hear what you're saying about laws . . . (I've forgotten your name.)

John John.

Colin I hear what you're saying, John, about names.

John Laws.

Colin What?

John About laws.

Colin Exactly – what did I say? – exactly. But what matters, John – as you so rightly point out – is freedom, freedom of choice. And every so-called law is by definition a restriction of that freedom. It's reducing in the very broadest sense the products that are available to me. You see I'm afraid I can understand crime. I can put myself in that man's mind. I can see the process . . .

John (This is the process of thought.)

Colin (Exactly.) . . . which brought it about.

Silence.

John What I don't understand is mindlessness. Can you understand that?

Colin Mindlessness? No. (In fact I don't think anyone . . .)

John Let's say it's some kid. And let's face it: it could be yours, it could be mine. Because this affects us all.

Colin This is mindlessness.

John And this kid, he goes into a shop and what he does is he purchases a can of aerosol paint and he sprays the letters C-U-N-T.

Colin Cunt.

John In a nutshell, he sprays that word on the side of a police vehicle.

Colin Right.

,

John Well you tell me, you tell me what's going on in that boy's mind.

Colin So you're – what – police?

John (That's right.) You tell me what's going on in his mind.

,

Colin I don't have the answer.

John Things which to me are a mental / illness.

Colin You're right. It's mindless.

John You see, I don't know what I would do if I didn't have faith.

Colin You have faith.

John I do.

Colin Well I admire that.

John I've thought about it and I think I would despair.

Colin gives John a piece of paper.

You're never tempted?

Colin What? To despair? (*faint laugh*)

John The Masonic Hall.

Colin Yes. Where is that – the Masonic Hall?

John You need to be there now?

Colin I need to be there tonight.

John What are you doing there?

Colin Where is that exactly?

John The station. It's near the station.

Colin takes back the paper. Silence.

Colin The police station?

John The railway station.

22

Colin Thank you. Is this old?

John Parts of it are old. Parts of it date back.

Colin Is that right? Which parts?

John I've no idea. So what is it you're doing there?

Colin (Sorry?) Depths. I'm doing depths.

Blackout.

1.3 MASONIC HALL

Liz and Colin (sober, alert, charming). Silence.

Colin In your own words.

Liz Well there's one where . . .

Colin Good.

Liz Where they're driving along in the car and they're having an argument – it's in some kind of desert – perhaps it's the Nevada desert – because you feel – although it's never stated – but you feel that this is America . . .

Colin i.e. they're in the United States . . .

Liz You feel they're (that's right) that they're in the United States and they're having an argument as I say and she stops the car and one of them gets out . . .

'

Is this what you mean?

Colin This is exactly what I mean.

Liz One of them gets out – it's him – and she drives off and he runs over the rocks – it's a rocky landscape – he drives over the rocks . . .

Colin Runs.

Liz That's right, he runs (what did I say?) over the rocks and somehow he's suddenly in front of the car, and it turns out that he's forgotten his jeans.

Colin He's forgotten his jeans.

Liz Or something. He's forgotten some denim article. A jacket, or . . .

Colin Uh-huh.

'

Good. Do you recall the brand?

Liz I'm sorry?

Colin What brand is that?

Liz I couldn't tell you. One of the big names.

Colin Which are the big names?

Liz I couldn't tell you the brand.

Colin Which are the big names?

Liz Well you *know* the big names.

Colin Imagine I don't.

Liz Why? (*faint laugh*)

Colin OK.

Liz Why d'you want me to do that?

Colin OK, what adjective would you use to describe this commercial?

Liz Which adjective?

Colin Give me (that's right) give me an adjective.

Liz Um . . . Puerile.

Colin Puerile. OK. Any others?

Liz What, which I . . .? (I mean not meaning other adjectives.)

Colin No (that's right) which you recall, others which you recall seeing nowadays.

Liz There is one . . .

Colin Good.

Liz One where . . . There's a housewife, and she . . . I mean she appears to be newly married. She's young and she's decorating. The house is white. The interior of their house is completely white. And some people arrive, I think these are relatives and they want some coffee. (Unexpectedly – I mean she's not prepared.) So the woman goes into her kitchen which is completely white and while she's making the coffee she produces a noise.

Colin Uh-huh. A noise.

Liz The noise is to deceive her relatives. (*faint laugh*)

Colin Uh-huh. Good. What about?

Liz About the nature of the coffee.

Colin The nature of the coffee. Why does she want to do that?

Liz You tell me.

Both faint laugh.

Colin I suspect from your tone . . .

Liz I have a tone?

Colin . . . that you also consider this puerile.

Liz Well I'm sorry.

Colin No, that's OK.

Liz I mean if I have a tone.

Liz looks at the camera.

You're recording this.

Colin Right. Yes. I should've explained. Sorry. I am. You're quite right. I do this (forgive me) I do this in order not to take notes. No one sees the videotape apart from myself. It just helps me recall your reactions.

Liz To what?

Colin To whatever. So don't feel inhibited.

Liz I'm not inhibited. I just suspect I'm not the kind of person who will say the right things.

Colin What right things? Listen, let me just establish something: there's no right or wrong in this.

Liz OK.

Colin OK?

Both faint laugh.

Let's talk about when your family comes in. In your own words.

Liz OK. Well in the week Jo gets home at about 4.30.

Colin Good. Describe to me in your own words what Jo does when he gets home.

Liz Jo is my daughter.

Colin Daughter. Good. What does – I stand corrected – what does Jo do when she gets home nowadays?

Liz Well the first thing she does is is she goes up to her room and changes out of her uniform . . .

Colin This is a school uniform . . .

Liz She changes (that's right) out of her school uniform and puts on her own things.

Colin How old is Jo?

Liz Jo is fifteen.

Colin OK.

Liz Although in fact . . .

Colin Right . . .

Liz Before she does that . . .

Colin Puts on her things . . .

Liz Before she puts on her things she generally washes her hair.

Colin OK.

Liz Because she comes home on the bus, and on the bus her friends all smoke. This isn't advertising cigarettes is it by the way? Because I would feel very strongly about that.

Colin Listen. Let me tell you exactly what this is not: this is not advertising, this is not selling.

,

Liz OK.

Colin OK? What products does she use to wash her hair?

Liz You'd have to ask her that.

Colin OK. (*They laugh.*) She buys her / own things.

Liz She buys her own / things.

Colin So you in fact give her / money.

Liz That's right. My husband, in fact it's my husband gives her an allowance for those things.

Colin What time does your husband come home?

Liz He doesn't come home.

Colin That's unfortunate.

Liz No what I mean is is he is already there.

Colin He works at / home.

Liz He works at home.

Colin What does he do?

Liz He's a writer.

Colin What does he write?

Liz He'd like to write –

Colin I'm sure, but what does he write?

Liz He'd like to write – I'm actually trying to tell you – write fiction. But since Jo was born he's been writing technical manuals for computer software . . .

Colin OK.

Liz Which he despises.

Colin So Jo has come in. She's washed her hair. (I don't see why he should despise that.) She's changed her clothes. Now what?

,

In your own words.

Liz (What?) Sorry.

Colin What does Jo do now? What I'm getting at is (and I don't want to prompt you here) but can we assume she now has a snack?

Liz That's right. She has her tea.

Colin Well thank God for that. (*Both laugh.*) What kind of snack?

Liz She has a pizza.

Colin Good. She has a pizza. Who cooks it?

Liz I do.

Colin Describe what you do.

Liz (*with irony*) In my own words.

Colin Naturally.

,

Liz Well all I do is is I take the pizza out of the freezer and I –

Colin Let me stop you a moment. Is it in a package?

Liz Well it was in a box, but before I put them in the freezer, I throw away the boxes to make more space. I don't like throwing them away, and I always tell myself that next time I'll find some . . . alternative. But whenever the moment comes I just think what the hell and I find myself doing it.

Colin This worries you.

Liz Not particularly. I mean it doesn't keep me awake at night.

,

So when I take it out it's not in a box but it's still wrapped in a plastic skin which I split this skin open with my teeth. I ought to use scissors but I split it with my teeth and maybe that's why sometimes fragments, because I've noticed that sometimes small fragments of cheese fall off at this point. (I'm sure you don't want to hear about this.)

Colin Does that bother you?

Liz (What?) No, as I say, they're only very small fragments.

Colin OK.

Liz So then I . . . Shall I / go on?

Colin Please go on.

Liz I put it in a pre-heated oven.

Colin This is a conventional / oven.

Liz A pre-heated conventional oven until it's cooked.

Colin Do you serve it accompanied by anything?

Liz No. On its own. But – one thing I do – before I cook it, I sometimes add extra cheese.

Colin That's interesting. Why do you do that?

Liz I would've thought that was obvious.

Colin I'd like to hear it in your own words.

Liz Simply because there is sometimes – well I feel – that there is insufficient cheese.

Colin That's very interesting. Is insufficient cheese as you call it generally a problem nowadays?

Liz I wouldn't call it a problem, no. (*faint laugh*)

'

I was told this would be about shopping.

Colin This is about shopping. Broadly. I'm interested in this use of a conventional oven. I take it you don't have a microwave oven?

Liz Paul – my husband – he would be against that.

Colin Why would he be against that? That's interesting. What would he be against?

Liz He would just be against it. (I can't really put this into words. I'm sorry.)

Colin OK. Try.

Liz I just mean (you know what I mean) that neither of us really believes in what that represents.

Colin What does it represent? No, that's interesting. What does it represent? Because I didn't know you could 'believe' in a microwave oven.

Liz I think you know what I mean.

Colin I'd like to hear it in your own words.

Liz I think you know what I mean.

,

Colin What does it / represent?

Liz Because as Paul says . . .

Colin This is what Paul says . . .

Liz Yes . . .

Colin Because I don't want to know what Paul says. What I want to know is what do *you* say, what do *you* think?

,

We can come back to that. Why don't you tell me some more about these small fragments of cheese?

31

Liz (You're joking.)

Colin i.e. is the cheese that you add cheese to *replace* as it were these fragments, or are you saying you would add cheese anyway?

,

In your own words.

,

Why am I joking?

Liz Listen.

Colin Good.

Liz Listen.

Colin That's fine.

Liz I ought to tell you something . . .

Colin Which is . . .

Liz I'm lying.

Colin You're lying.

,

Good. No. Sorry. Elucidate. What, you mean you're some kind of pathological . . .?

Liz (I'm sorry.)

Colin Meaning what: you're lying? What about? About the cheese? Why?

Liz Not about the cheese.

Colin Not the cheese.

Liz I no longer live with my husband.

Colin Paul. The writer.

Liz I no longer live (– that's right, with Paul.)

Colin Jesus wept. As of when?

Liz It's a week now, and from your point of view it may not be relevant but lying makes me . . . I'm beginning to feel uncomfortable about lying – 'Paul does this, Paul does that' –

Colin Why are you lying?

Liz I don't know. I don't know, but I just want to clear that up before we go on.

Colin It's not possible to go on.

Liz (Because as far as the household is concerned . . .)

Colin I'll tell you something: you no longer have a household. A household for our purposes consists of certain elements, i.e. we're talking either husband or, failing husband, income. From what I gather, you have neither – which my heart goes out to you – but it's not possible to go on and I've just lost fifteen per cent of my sample on that account.

,

These are AB women. I generally get integrity from AB women.

Liz Integrity . . .

Colin Yes.

Liz . . . just seems a strange word to use in this context.

Colin Well I'm sorry, I'm terribly sorry but whichever word you use I still have a client who expects to see not five but six videos of AB women reacting to his product.

Liz You told me no one would see the tape.

Colin Did I? (Well maybe in the heat of the moment . . .)

He laughs and shakes his head.

Did I really tell you that? Because that's not true, that just isn't true.

Silence.

Liz Look, I'll just go.

Colin Please don't go.

Liz looks at the camera.

Liz Is this still on?

Colin I'm sorry. Yes.

Colin turns off the tape, looks at his watch.

We still have forty minutes. Can I buy you a drink?

Liz You're joking.

,

I mean you must be / joking.

Colin (*calls*) Karen.

,

Are you expecting him back?

Liz I thought we'd finished.

,

No. No, I'm not.

Colin Uh-huh.

Silence. Karen appears.

Karen Hello?

Colin Karen, will you please get this lady her envelope.

Karen goes.

Clearly you have a problem with this.

Liz Me? I don't have a problem.

Colin OK. Good. That's just as well, because this is – what's wrong with this? – because this is, after all, this is it, this is our culture.

Liz It's not mine.

Colin That's a shame.

Liz It's not my culture.

Colin Which is a shame.

,

No, that really is a shame, because an idea enters my head, and the idea is –

Liz What idea?

Colin The idea is – it enters my head just now looking at you – and it is that I could employ you.

Liz laughs.

Colin (*laughs*) I'm serious. I could employ you. That is within my power.

Liz If you think I'm going to stand out on the street –

Colin Not on the street. No. To do what I do. You could do (if you liked) what I do. That is within my power.

,

Don't decide immediately.

Liz I don't need to decide.

Colin It may not be what (obviously) you want.

35

Liz It's not what I / want.

Colin So what do you want? I'm just saying (and I would suggest you give this some thought) that I could do this for you. As a friend.

Liz I don't need to decide.

Colin Well I respect that.

Karen approaches with an envelope.

Liz Because when you say culture all I see is . . . nothing . . . it's about nothing . . . these questions . . . all you can say about it is what it isn't . . . it's a void, you're creating a void.

Colin I'm creating a void.

Liz Well don't you think so?

Colin Uh-huh. Thank you.

'

Thank you. Because it seems to me (is that so?) that I am in fact doing the opposite. Wouldn't you say, Karen? That our job is not to create, it's to fill, it's to fill the void.

'

That's what we're doing here.

Liz What's this?

Karen This is your gift.

Liz I don't want that, thank you.

Colin Like it or not.

Liz I really don't want that.

Blackout.

36

Act Two

2.1 HOME

Jo and Liz.

Jo is drying her hair with a towel. She wears a man's shirt.

Jo Where've you been?

Liz Shopping.

,

Jo Paul rang.

Liz Did he.

,

What about?

Jo He didn't say anything, he just rang. But I know it was him, because it was his kind of silence.

,

I mean the kind where you don't even hear any breathing.

Both faint laugh.

You don't think he's going to ask for his clothes, do you, because I really like wearing his clothes.

,

When will we see him, will we see him at weekends?

,

No, we were talking about it and Marianne said maybe
it's because you married young – she said that can
happen, if you both marry young, and then the man . . .

'

I'm sorry.

Liz How was school?

Jo School was good. (I'm sorry.)

Liz Good.

Jo No, it was good. We did the golden age.

Liz What's that?

Jo Holland in the golden age.

Liz What's that?

Jo History.

'

The golden age, it's just when everybody is tremendously
wealthy and confident and . . . they like paintings and
they're really optimistic about the future . . . And at the
same time they really care, they really do care about the
poor, whatever, meaning that they build poorhouses
where poor people can work . . .

Liz Uh-huh . . .

Jo . . . spin or make sawdust.

Liz gradually stops paying attention.

And they had this place where if you *didn't* work they
put you in this place, a kind of cell under the ground
and flooded it with water where there was a pump, so
what you had to do was pump and you would be OK.
But one day there was this guy and they put this guy

who wouldn't work (I mean some kind of total misfit)
put him in this place and started flooding it, and what
happened was he wouldn't pump. (*faint laugh*) I mean
he died, he drowned, and that really confused them, the
burghers. (We're doing a project on it.)

,

What're you doing?

Liz I thought I'd put an envelope on here.

Jo What kind of envelope?

Liz An envelope with money in it.

Jo And Jason said, what kind of fucking idiot would do
that? (*laughs*) He actually said fucking. It was brilliant.

Liz Have you seen it?

Jo What?

Liz The envelope.

,

Jo That was weeks ago.

,

I used your conditioner. Smell.

Liz Why?

Jo It's got that oil in it, that South American oil. It
smells good.

Liz Why did you do that?

Jo It says on the bottle this South American oil (why
d'you think?) comes from a rare white flower which
opens its petals just before dusk.

Liz You've got your own.

39

Jo It's run out.

,

That's where I'd like to be. I'd like to be that flower.

Liz Please buy your own in future.

Jo What with, Elizabeth?

Liz Has anyone called?

Jo I told you who called.

Liz Has anyone else called?

Jo You mean your friend?

Liz He's not my friend.

,

He's not my / friend.

Jo I thought he was your / friend.

Liz I just asked if he called.

Jo No.

Liz Thank you. Look, d'you mind getting your own snack?

Jo What is that: my snack?

Liz Your snack. Your tea. D'you mind / getting it?

Jo What sort of word is that? You've never said snack. Paul never said / snack.

Liz I'm not interested in what Paul never said. You can use whatever word you like but will you please get it.

,

Jo OK.

Liz I'm just going upstairs.

Jo (Snack. Why not?)

Liz I'm just going up to his room . . .

Jo (Snack. Snack is fine. Snack.)

Liz I want to clear out the papers up there . . .

Jo (I can adjust.)

Liz Clear them out and burn them. It's a mess up there.

Jo You can't burn his things.

Liz I can burn – listen to me, Joanna – I can burn whatever I like. I don't think I'm going to sleep properly until those things are out. And besides we need the room, both of us could do with the room, with the space, I've made up my mind.

Jo He might want them. What if he needs those things? What if he comes back and he needs those things?

Liz He's not coming back here. There's no question of that. I've told you: I've made up my mind. And what we need now is space, is room. I've got some black plastic sacks. I may want you to help me with the sacks. And if they won't – because I've been thinking about this and it's possible they'll be too thick – too thick to burn. So then we can just leave them, just leave them by the bins in those sacks. No. I want them out. I want those things out of here and I want you to help me.

Jo is crying. Liz goes to her, but is pushed away.

Jo This is so *embarrassing*. This is so *suburban*.

Silence.

Liz D'you think it slipped down the back of something?

Blackout.

2.2 A ROOM IN THE FEATHERS HOTEL

Colin, alone.

Waiting for a phone connection, Colin watches the videotape of his interview with Liz. We see her face in close-up. Dialogue preceeded by < is on video.

<Colin What does he do?

<Liz He's a writer.

<Colin What does he write?

<Liz He'd like to write –

<Colin I'm sure, but what does he write?

<Liz He'd like to write – I'm actually trying to tell you – write fiction. But since Jo was born he's been writing technical manuals for computer software . . .

<Colin OK.

<Liz Which he despises.

<Colin So Jo has come in. She's washed her hair. (I don't see why he should despise that.) She's changed her clothes. Now what?

,

In your own words.

<Liz (What?) Sorry.

<Colin What does Jo do now? What I'm getting at is (and I don't want to prompt you here) but can we assume she now has a snack?

<Liz That's right. She has her tea.

<Colin Well thank God for that. (*Both laugh.*)

42

Faint laugh from Colin in the room.

What kind of snack?

<Liz She has a pizza.

<Colin Good. She has a pizza. Who cooks it?

<Liz I do.

<Colin Describe what you do.

<Liz In my own words.

<Colin Naturally.

Faint laugh from Colin in the room.

<Liz Well all I do is is I take the pizza / out of the freezer and I –

Colin Let me stop you a moment.

<Colin Let me stop you a moment. Is it in a package?

<Liz Well it was in a box, but before I put them in the freezer, I throw away the boxes to make more space. I don't like throwing them away, and I always tell myself that next time I'll find some . . .

Colin Alternative.

<Liz . . . alternative. But whenever the moment comes I just think what the hell and I find myself / doing it.

Colin This worries you.

<Colin This worries you.

<Liz Not particularly. I mean it doesn't keep me awake at night.

,

Colin So when I take it out.

43

<Liz So when I take it out it's not in a box but it's still wrapped in a plastic skin which I split this skin open with my teeth. I ought to use scissors but I split it with my teeth and maybe that's why sometimes fragments, because I've noticed that sometimes small fragments –

Colin freezes the tape as he speaks into the phone. A blurred image of Liz's face remains on the screen.

Colin (*into phone*) Not as sorry as I am, my love. Would it be technologically possible to get me an outside line, please.

He dials. Outside the hotel, in the distance, a brief dull metallic vibration.

Hello. This is me.
Hello.
I'm very well. I wondered if you had reached a decision.
You're still thinking. Well I respect that.
I have the utmost respect for that. Because I am the same (believe it or not) as yourself. No one is going to tell me what to do, what to think. I'm one hundred per cent on your wavelength, and so I don't want you to feel pressured.
I don't want you to feel pressured in any way. All I'm saying is, is as I've said before, and I'll say it again, it would be very good news to have you with us, but that is entirely your choice. Did I get you out of bed by the way?
Out of bed. Because I'm just looking at my watch here and I notice that it's – Jesus wept, it's one o'clock in the morning. How did that happen? Listen I'm sorry.
Are you sure? It's OK? Because suddenly I have an image of you . . .
What do I mean? I just mean (exactly what I say) that I have an image of you.

Distant metallic sound.

Me? No. I'm in the North East. I'm doing groups in the North East.

A group? A group is the same thing as a depth only there are more of them. Free wine. Yours truly. They love it. (*laughs*) One thing I've noticed is that spring is much later up here, because here I am in the Feathers Hotel and there is some kind of blossom outside the window.

Yes. Floodlit, I spent a while in the bar, and I can tell you there are some real characters. There are some real characters here in the North East.

Of course you would manage. I've told you: this is an executive position. Skill doesn't come into it. Just acquaint yourself with the vocabulary, and the rest will follow.

Feminine hygiene. The one I have in mind for you is feminine hygiene. Perfectly straightforward depths. There's just a remote possibility that there would be a client.

Just meaning that some interfering fuck of a client wants to see what he stroke she is paying for. (I've told them it's out of the question.) You would manage.

What do I want? (Well thank you.) You mean do I have designs on your . . . I mean am I breathing in a particular way, or . . . (*laughs*)

Be serious? Wouldn't that be serious? (Alright. Be serious. What do I want? That's difficult. Because people talk about behaviour and motives and so on, and the *reason* for what is going on here.) Or perhaps I have an image of what I want, mentally, but outside of that there's nothing the image corresponds to. So all I would ask from you (I know – it's late) are two things, that is, A, your report, and naturally your invoice.

B? B is the invoice. Sorry. (*faint laugh*) So listen, if the answer is yes what I'll do is I can come to you on the day because you'll need some stimulus material for the warm-up.

i.e. these are magazines.

That's right. I could come to you, come to your house, bring this material, and talk you through. Then afterwards I would be there to discuss any problem.

I'm not assuming anything, Elizabeth.

Distant metallic sound.

It sounds very quiet there.

Isn't she? What, is she out on the town?

Isn't she? Well maybe she can't get to a phone (or doesn't want to). Listen, I ought to go. I'll speak to you soon. Why don't you make yourself a hot drink?

That's what I always do. I always make myself a nice hot drink, and in two minutes I'm dead to the world. I need to know soon.

Yes. Speak to you soon. Goodnight.

He hangs up, switches off the video.

Blackout.

2.3 MASONIC HALL

Liz and Sally.

They are watched by Roger, the client.

Liz In your own words.

Sally How d'you mean, what kind of car?

Liz Right. Sorry. How can I explain? Well let's say it was . . . restaurants.

Sally Restaurants.

Liz Then if it was restaurants, then Maxim's you could call a Rolls-Royce.

Sally What's Maxim's?

Liz It's a smart restaurant in Paris.

Sally So then it should be a Citroen.

Liz Sorry? Yes. That's very good.

Sally Cos it should be French.

Liz That's excellent. And a chip shop, that could be . . .

Sally Something greasy.

Liz Fine. It could be, I don't know, an Escort, a Ford Escort.

Sally OK. I'm with you.

Sally picks out some magazines.

Right then. *Cosmo*, that's . . . Well it's not a Roller . . . it's more of a . . . I'd call it a BMW.

Liz Why would you call it a BMW?

Sally What, d'you think that's wrong?

Liz Not at all.

Sally Cos I may be wrong. And *Jackie* . . . well *Jackie*'s not a car at all.

Liz It's not a car.

Sally No, *Jackie*'s more a kind of moped.

Liz Good.

Sally Well don't you think I'm right?

Liz There's no right answer.

Sally And *Woman's Weekly* . . . (*laughs*)

Liz Is that funny?

Sally Yeah.

Liz Why is it funny?

Sally Well don't you think it's funny? I'll tell you what that is, it's a T-reg Ford Cortina, OK, and it's got this miserable-looking family in it and they've all got on these hand-knitted jumpers and they're going to visit someone in hospital. They've got these cakes for them in a plastic box what they've made themselves, the cakes.

Liz Fine.

    Sally looks at the camera.

Sally Can I ask you a question?

Liz Of course.

Sally Am I on video?

Liz Yes. Sorry. I should've said.

Sally That's brilliant. Will I get to see it? I mean will this be on TV?

Liz No.

Sally Cos if it's on TV, y'know, my friends would like to see it. When does it go out?

Liz It won't be on TV. No one will see the tape apart from / myself.

Sally Shall I tell you what I really like?

Liz Yes. Good. Provided it's / relevant.

Sally I really like – when you're on the tube – I really like going down the end of the platform where you can see yourself in the camera.

Liz OK. Good. Perhaps we could / get back to . . .

Sally Y'know, because there is a camera down there for the driver and you can see yourself in it on the screen only it's yellow. That's a real laugh. And by the way if this is a survey what I want to know is why whenever you put any money in a chocolate machine you don't get any chocolate out – will you ask them that?

Liz OK. We really ought to get back / to . . .

Sally The other thing is electrical stores, I mean like Dixon's and Lasky's where they put a camera in the window and what you can do is see yourself in the video actually in the shop. Cos my uncle hired one for my cousin's eighteenth and we've got this really brilliant video of the disco and everything which I'm in it.

Liz That's very good.

Sally Although mainly my cousin.

Liz Fine.

Sally Trish.

Liz OK. Fine.

Sally She reads *Cosmo*.

Liz Does she? That's very good. If we could just get back to . . .

    Liz consults her notes.

Sally Can I ask you a question?

Liz Of course.

Sally Who is that bloke?

Liz Yes. I'm sorry. That's Roger.

Sally Roger.

Liz Yes, he's just . . .

Sally Hello, Roger.

Liz Roger is just here to observe.

Roger raises a hand in acknowledgement.

OK, so let me move on and ask you what advertising you can recall for sanitary products nowadays?

Sally How d'you mean, sanitary?

Liz Just in your own words.

Sally You mean like tampons?

Liz That's right.

Sally Can I remember any ads?

Liz That's right.

Sally Yea, there's one (yeah, I can) there's one where it's in this glass.

Liz Good.

Sally You can see it in this glass.

,

Liz Good. What d'you think that ad is trying to tell you about the product?

Sally Well that it fits you, y'know.

,

Liz That it fits you. Uh-huh.

Sally Yeah, that it fits you inside so you won't have to worry.

Liz Is that something you do?

Sally Worry?

Liz Yes.

Sally No.

,

Can I just get this right: this is about shopping?

Liz Broadly.

Sally OK.

,

Liz Who purchases these kinds of products in your household nowadays?

Sally What? For me? Well my mum used to, but since I've started working full-time, now I shop for myself mostly.

Liz What d'you do?

Sally Where do I work? I work in Saxone's.

Liz Which is a shoe-shop.

Sally That's right. It's a shoe-shop, but it's one of the big names.

Liz So you've left school.

Sally Well y'know, fuck that, fuck school. I mean I want to *get* somewhere in life. (I'm not sitting there till I'm eighteen.) I can say that, can I?

Liz Say what?

Sally I can say that on the video?

Liz Fuck? Why not?

Sally OK.

,

51

(OK. Yeah. I buy them myself.) Is that what you mean?

Liz Tell me about your first period, Sally.

Sally How d'you mean: about it?

Liz Just in your own words.

,

Just whatever you may recall in your own words.

Sally Well . . . I just remember my mum. The first time –
it was the next day – she said to me – my mum – and I
don't know why but I sat on her lap – and that was
funny – you know as a thing, a thing to do – I sat on her
lap and she said, you've started your period, Sal, you're
not my little girl any more.

,

That's all she said.

,

Liz Good.

Sally Can I ask you a question?

Liz Of course.

Sally I mean does Roger get off on this or something?

Liz I should've explained.

Sally Do you, Roger?

Liz I should've explained that Roger is my client. He's
just here to observe.

Roger raises hand as before.

Please don't feel inhibited.

Sally I'm not inhibited.

Liz OK.

Sally I'm not inhibited.

Liz That's good.

,

That's very / good.

Sally I'm not inhibited, I'm just asking what he is *into*, y'know.

Liz It's just his job.

Sally Like this is your job.

Liz Exactly the same.

,

OK?

Sally OK.

Liz You use a product with an applicator, is that right?

Sally Yup.

Liz Can you tell me why you choose to do that?

Sally It's more convenient.

,

Liz Good. What makes it more convenient?

,

That's very good. We can come back to that. Let me ask you, what does TSS mean to you?

Sally Nothing.

Liz OK, if I tell you that stands for Toxic Shock Syndrome . . .

Sally What's that?

Liz That's fine. Good.

Liz gets up.

Sally What *is* that?

Liz What I want, what I'm going to do now, Sally, is I'm just going to show you some ideas for various products.

Sally What is that thing you said?

Roger It will emerge.

Liz Yes, as Roger says, it will emerge in the course of the concepts.

Sally I mean if you're trying to sell me something, why don't you just tell me what it is you're trying to sell me?

Roger We're not trying to sell you anything, Sally.

Liz No. That's right, that's absolutely right. I should've said (thank you) that this is not – OK? – because I ought to tell you right now that this is not selling, this is not advertising.

Blackout.

2.4 HOME

Colin and Jo.

Silence. Jo runs a hand through her hair.

Colin Your mother does that.

Jo What?

,

Colin Do I call you Jo or Joanna?

Jo Whichever.

Colin I like that kind of name.

Jo What kind of name is that?

   Both faint laugh. Silence.

Don't you answer questions?

Colin Um . . . Yes.

   Both faint laugh.

It's light now in the evenings.

Jo Elizabeth had a fire out there.

Colin Did she?

Jo It's made the grass black.

,

It's really suburban here.

Colin Does that word have a meaning?

Jo It means (yes) it means all the television aerials are
pointing in the same direction.

Colin Where would you like to be?

Jo Wherever.

,

I know some people, and they're living on a bus.

Colin Are they?

Jo I don't mean hippies, because they are organised.

Colin D'you smoke?

Jo No thanks.

Colin lights up.

Jo I'd like to be mobile. I'd like to have my own car.

Colin Where would you go?

Jo What?

,

Into the country.

Colin Would you?

Jo I'd go into the country.

Colin Why?

Jo Why? Why not? (*faint laugh*)

,

Because I like trees, and I like stars. I like the dark. It's never dark here.

Colin Why not?

Jo Because of the lights.

Colin Why do you like stars?

Jo Why do I like stars?

Jo looks at Colin and begins to laugh. They laugh together.

I've got a friend and sometimes – this is my friend drives me into the country, and we do things like (I don't know why I'm telling you this) like a few nights ago we just pulled off the road somewhere – this was in the middle of the night – and walked into a field. It was scary. I never knew the stars had different colours. (*faint laugh*) I got home incredibly late and I'd ruined my shoes.

Colin Why did it scare you?

Jo I suppose . . . I suppose it made me feel like a different kind of person.

Colin What kind of person?

Jo faint laugh.

I'm sorry.

Jo I feel as if I'm being . . .

Colin What?

Jo Questioned.

Colin Why d'you feel that?

Both laugh.

I'm sorry. I'm probing.

Jo (I know.) Are you? What d'you mean, probing?

Colin It's my job. Probing. Probing is a technical term. It means eliciting a response.

Jo And that's your job?

Colin You can probe or you can prompt. Trust the former, avoid the latter. Probing is 'Why do you like stars?' Prompting is 'Why do you like stars? Is it by any chance because their remote and mysterious colours make you feel like a different kind of person?' Which is to be avoided.

Jo That's what Elizabeth's doing?

Colin Yes, but not about stars.

Jo fiddles with her necklace. Silence.

Jo Could I do it?

Colin What?

Jo Could I do it to you?

Colin Do what to me, sorry?

Jo Could I have a cigarette now?

Colin Do what, exactly, to me?

He gives her a cigarette.

Um . . . Meaning what?

Jo Ask you questions.

Colin What sort of questions? You're joking. (*faint laugh*) I'm afraid you must be joking.

He lights her cigarette.

Jo What's your name?

Colin Come on, come on . . . I have not agreed to this.

Jo What's your name?

Colin Colin. My name is Colin, but listen, I have not agreed –

Jo No. I mean your full name.

Colin What?

Jo Your full name.

Colin It's Parker. Colin Parker. OK? (Can we leave this?)

Jo Is that your real name?

Colin Meaning what exactly?

Jo It doesn't sound real.

Colin Well I'm terribly sorry.

Jo Is it real?

Colin Of course it's real. (Jesus wept.)

Jo How old are you?

Colin What?

Jo How old are you?

Colin Thirty.

,

I'm thirty-two.

Jo I thought you were older.

Colin I'm thirty-two years old.

Jo Are you married?

Colin Am I what?

Jo I'm probing.

Colin Very good.

Jo Are you married?

Colin Yes.

Jo What's your wife's name?

Colin (You're really probing.)

Jo Answer me.

Colin Jennifer. Her name is Jennifer. OK?

,

(You'll forgive me if I fail to see the / relevance . . .)

Jo Am I any good?

Colin Very good. You get the job.

Jo I don't want the job. Where do you and Jennifer live?

Colin (We live in the country.) I thought we'd stopped.

59

Jo I thought you lived round here.

Colin I've just told you where we live. We live in the country, on an estate.

Jo You mean a cottage?

Colin I don't mean a cottage, I mean what I said: an estate, a housing-estate.

Jo Don't you like it?

Colin That's prompting. I do like it. I like it very much. Don't prompt. Don't tell me what to think.

,

Jo Sorry.

Colin I like it very much, Jo. I live in a Chalfont. Do you know what a Chalfont is? A Chalfont, that has four bedrooms and an integral garage. It's similar to the Blenheim, only the Blenheim – although it has the double garage – it lacks, the essential difference is that it lacks the shower-room ensuite.

Jo Is that important?

Colin It's not important, but it's very convenient. Did I say it was important?

Jo So what do you do?

Colin In the house? (What do I do . . .?) I'll tell you one thing I do in the house and that's I play the drums.

Jo What, are you in a band?

Colin Not in a band. No. I have a room. I just have a room. My room. It has net curtains, and there's a drum-kit in it.

Ash falls from Jo's cigarette.

Jo Oh God, this is going on the carpet.

Jo fusses over the ash. She picks up the ashtray and stubs out her cigarette.

She'll have a fit.

Colin Perhaps you should put it down.

Jo Right. What? This. Yes.

Jo puts down the ashtray. Colin stubs out his cigarette.

I think it sounds horrible.

Colin What does?

'

OK, so you despise me.

Jo That's not what I / mean.

Colin I can see you despise me. And that's fine. At the moment you can afford to. But I'll tell you something: we all turn, Jo, into the kind of people we used to despise.

Jo I won't.

Jo fiddles with her necklace and becomes withdrawn. Silence. Eventually Colin clicks his fingers in front of her face. They both smile.

What?

Colin Nothing. That's pretty.

Jo This? They make them.

Colin On the bus.

Jo How did you know that?

Colin May I see?

Jo How did you know that?

Colin May I see it?

She passes him the necklace.

Jo That's right. They sell them in subways.

Colin Silver.

Jo That's right. It's silver and the stones are lapis lazuli.

Colin Your friend gave it to you.

Jo What friend?

Colin Your friend in the field.

Jo (*faint laugh*) No. I paid for it. Don't tell Elizabeth. She thinks it's a gift.

Colin holds up the necklace. Jo reaches for it.

Colin Let me.

Jo bows her head and Colin attempts to fasten the necklace.

Silence.

Jo Can't you do it?

Colin I bite my nails.

Liz (*off*) Hello!

Jo Hi.

Jo reaches round and fastens the necklace. Liz appears. She's holding a bottle of champagne.

Colin How did it go?

Liz (*with excitement*) You're looking at a natural. I was marvellous. I was wonderful. I had one girl and she was so difficult but I – like you said – I reassured her and I

62

got through it. The others were no problem at all, they were just with me all the way – will you get some glasses? And they responded to the cars, they really liked the idea of the cars (their imaginations . . .) and like you said, they *wanted* to talk, they in fact they enjoyed that, the chance to talk about themselves. It was just this one. I mean have you ever had one like that where they . . . I mean she was so aggressive . . . (*She pops the cork.*) . . . I mean actually rude to me (and to Roger) but I handled her and the fact is is I think I'm actually very *good* at it – will you get us some glasses, Jo . . .

Jo goes.

. . . because I think I have – well Roger was saying that I seem to have (d'you think he was telling the truth?) that I seem to have some kind of instinct, some kind of natural . . . empathy and at the end he just came up to me and he gave me this.

'

Was he not meant to do that?

Jo brings in two tumblers and leaves the room.

Because he thought it was very interesting, he thought I'd uncovered – although I said to him: look, it was quite unconscious – but that I'd uncovered a whole area, he in fact said this.

Colin Roger.

Liz Yes, that unconsciously or not I'd uncovered a whole area which no one has ever exploited. (*She fills the glasses.*) He couldn't believe it was my first time. Where's Jo? (*calls*) Jo.

Liz drinks.

(How's she been?)

63

Colin (Fine. She's been fine.)

Liz (*filling her glass*) She said to me 'Can I say that?'
I said to her 'Say what?'

Colin Did you?

Liz Can you guess what she meant?

Colin Guess? No. Elucidate.

Liz She meant fuck.

Colin I see.

Liz The girl, this girl, she meant fuck.

,

You're not drinking.

Colin I'm driving.

Liz So I just said to her 'Why not?'

,

Has something happened?

Colin Happened? Where? No. Listen, I have to / go.

Liz Have you got to go? You're not drinking.

Colin I've got to drive back to the country.

Liz Don't you want to go over this?

Colin It seems fine.

Liz I thought you wanted to go over this.

,

I thought you wanted to go over this. If you're worried
about driving, you can stay. Because there's a room. We
have a whole room now.

Colin I'm not worried about driving.

Liz There's a whole empty room.

Colin In fact I quite like driving.

Um . . . Invoice me.

Colin goes. Silence.

Liz (*calls*) Jo.

Silence.

(*calls*) Joanna.

Silence.

Fade.

Act Three

3.1 THE BAR OF THE FEATHERS HOTEL

April of the following year.
  Liz, Nigel, Paul. (Also Gary, who is not seen).
  Nigel is beside Liz at the bar. Her back is to the audience, and her responses to Nigel are hardly audible. Paul, a young man, sits watching them.

Nigel Shall I tell you what the trouble is?

,

I'll tell you what the trouble is: the trouble is is people are too mobile. They move around. Wherever you look there are people just moving around. They think because they move around they'll find happiness. And do they find happiness? No, they don't.

,

D'you know where my son is now? I say: d'you know where my son is now?

Liz (No.)

Nigel No. You don't. And neither do I. (*laughs*)

,

Because look at Gary over there. You're not looking. He's over there. That's Gary.

Liz (Gary.)

Nigel That's right. In the T-shirt. That's Gary. Now I'll tell you something about Gary. Gary comes here to the Feathers Hotel, he comes in here every night of his life. And d'you know what he does? Well do you?

66

Liz (I've no idea.)

Nigel raises the fingers of both hands.

Nigel That's what he does.

Liz (Really.)

Nigel That's what he does every night of his life. He comes in here and he has ten pints of ale each and every night of his life. What d'you say to that? I say: what d'you say to that?

Liz (Amazing.)

Nigel It's what?

Liz (It's amazing.)

Nigel You're right. It is amazing. Because, alright, he likes a drink, no one's saying otherwise, but what you're looking at is a stable family man.

Liz (He's married?)

Nigel Certainly he's married. Got two lovely little 'uns what come here with his wife Sunday lunchtimes because there is a garden for them. He was born here and he will die here, and his children were born here and they will die here. How many of us can honestly say that about ourselves?

,

Alright, so he likes a drink, who doesn't, but I tell you for a fact he walks out of here at a quarter to midnight with the same dignity as what he walked in here at half past six. What can I get you?

,

What can I get you to drink?

Liz (Nothing.)

Nigel Nothing? Why's that?

,

Why is that? Don't you answer questions?

,

Is that a medium dry?

Liz (I really don't want anything.)

Nigel Maybe you don't want anything, but the point is I'm offering. You're not from round here, are you?

,

Well are you?

Liz (I'm working here.)

Nigel You're working here. Doing what? Sounds very interesting. I don't think women should work, do you? This is nothing personal, I just don't think that they should. I think it's all wrong. I think they're too mobile. I think there's too much freedom and that's why nobody has a place, nobody has a role. Because there was a time when everybody knew their place and you can say what you like but the fact remains that they knew.

Liz (Like Gary.)

Nigel *Exactly* like Gary. There's nothing wrong with Gary. Alright, so he likes a drink, but he knows what he wants out of life, and how many of us can honestly say that about ourselves? You from London, then?

,

D'you know where my son is now? Of course you don't and neither do I. (*laughs*) We laugh about it.

Silence.

Have you seen *Cats*? I say: have you see *Cats*?

Liz (No.)

Nigel Haven't you? Why not? My wife wants to see it for our silver wedding. Gary's been down on the coach and he says it's a load of crap. What do you think?

Liz (I haven't seen it.)

Nigel Alright, so you haven't seen it, but you must have an opinion.

,

I read this article and it said in this article how there are women in offices down there as can earn two hundred pound a day. I said to my wife it says here there are women in offices as can earn two hundred pound a day. She said to me – and this'll make you laugh – she said 'Don't talk to me about offices there's no bloody women what earn a thousand pound a week unless it's flat on their backs like.' Flat on their backs, we had a good laugh about that.

> *Liz throws her drink in his face. Paul stands, as if he might intervene. On seeing this, Nigel silently withdraws. Liz starts to move away, but Paul speaks.*

Paul Can I –

Liz Buy me a drink? Buy me lunch? Give me a lift somewhere?

,

Paul I don't have a car.

> *They both laugh. They look at each other.*
> *Blackout.*

3.2 MASONIC HALL

Colin and Karen.

They've finished work and are watching a tape of Sally's interview with Liz. Sally's face appears in close-up. Dialogue preceded by < indicates on video.

<Liz Of course.

<Sally Am I on video?

<Liz Yes. Sorry. I should've said.

<Sally That's brilliant. Will I get to see it? I mean will this be on TV?

<Liz No.

<Sally Cos if it's on TV, y'know, my friends would like to see it. When does it go out?

<Liz It won't be on TV. No one will see the tape apart from / myself.

Colin and Karen laugh.

<Sally Shall I tell you what I really like?

<Liz Yes. Good. Provided it's / relevant.

<Sally I really like – when you're on the tube – I really like going down the end of the platform where you can see yourself in the camera.

<Liz OK. Good. Perhaps we could / get back to . . .

<Sally Y'know, because there is a camera down there for the driver . . .

Karen (*laughs*) Where did you *find* this?

<Sally . . . and you can see yourself in it on the screen

only it's yellow. That's a real laugh. And by the way if
this is a survey what I want to know is why whenever
you put any money in a chocolate machine you don't get
any chocolate out – will you ask them that?

<Liz OK. We really ought to get back / to . . .

Colin and Karen laugh.

<Sally The other thing is electrical stores, I mean like
Dixon's and Lasky's where they put a camera in the
window and what you can do is see yourself in the video
actually in the shop. Cos my uncle hired one for my
cousin's eighteenth and we've got this really brilliant
video of the disco and everything which I'm in it.

<Liz That's very good.

<Sally Although mainly my cousin.

<Liz Fine.

<Sally Trish.

<Liz OK. Fine.

<Sally She reads *Cosmo*.

*Karen continues to laugh as Colin turns off and ejects
the tape.*

Karen Where did you *find* that?

Colin It's just a project from last year. It should've been
wiped.

Karen There's a message from your wife.

Colin unfolds the piece of paper and reads in silence.

Colin Did you take this message?

Karen No. Someone out the back.

Colin Someone out the back.

Karen Yes. Is it bad news?

Colin Read it. Read it to me.

Karen We need frozen peas.

Colin We need frozen peas. Very bad news. Say my name, Karen.

Karen What?

Colin Say my name. Speak it.

Karen Speak it?

Colin Speak my name.

Karen Colin?

Colin The whole name. Speak my whole name.

Karen Colin Parker.

Colin Exactly. (Thank you.) Does it sound real?

Karen Real?

Colin Does it sound real to you?

Karen Will you need me tomorrow?

Colin (It sounds real to me.)

Karen Do you need me on / Saturday?

Colin On Saturday. No.

Karen Because I'd like Monday off.

Colin What has that to do with Saturday, with tomorrow?

Karen I would've said, can I have Monday for Saturday, that was assuming –

Colin Why is that? Why would you like Monday off?

,

Why is that? I'm just / curious.

Karen A friend of mine has killed herself.

Colin Uh-huh. OK. That's fine.

,

Did she? Because that's absolutely fine by me.

Karen Thank you.

Colin Why did she do that?

Karen Why don't you ask her?

Colin Monday. (Point taken.) Monday is actually a difficult day. Don't we have groups on Monday?

Karen I know.

Colin It has to be Monday? There's no way of / changing . . .

Karen I'm sorry.

Colin So is that a.m. or p.m.?

Karen I'm sorry, it's both. I have to travel.

Colin Jesus wept.

,

You know that kind of thing actually pisses me off. It's the void. D'you know what I mean by the void? The void, that is, 'There is no meaning to my life' or 'We are no longer in touch with what is real' or 'We have lost a dimension and in its place we are confronted by a capital V void which cannot be filled,' You're grieving – I'm sorry – but the void pisses me off, Karen. It pisses me off utterly. 'It's dark in the void. It's cold in the void. We're alone here in the void.' (*with fury*) Because fuck that, did I invent it? Did I invent the void?

'

(You're grieving. I'm sorry. Monday is fine.)

Karen (Thank you.)

Colin Because there are benefits and we are surrounded by them.

   Silence.

Tell me what's happening, Karen.

Karen We've finished here with the blend.

Colin OK.

Karen And Liz is also taking groups tonight in the North East.

Colin On the blend. Is she?

Karen On the blend, yes. And Roger . . .

Colin (Don't talk to me about Roger.)

Karen Roger would like to see something before Monday.

Colin Videotapes.

Karen Videotapes.

Colin Before Monday.

Karen I ought to / go.

Colin Please don't go.

'

Your heart isn't in this, is it.

Karen Sorry? My heart? (*faint laugh*)

Colin An expression. You do know that expression?

Karen Yes.

Colin Well?

Karen What?

Colin Is it?

Karen Is it what?

Colin I feel you're critical.

Karen Critical of what? (I'm sorry . . .)

Colin I feel you're standing back, Karen. I don't feel you're with us.

Karen I don't follow.

Colin I feel you're saying 'This isn't me'.

Karen I don't follow you.

Colin Because what have we here? What we have is an intelligent person who seems content to put money in envelopes when you could do what I do.

Karen I don't want to do what you do.

Colin I want to know why.

Karen There's no reason.

Colin That's not an answer.

Karen There isn't an answer – what you call an answer.

Colin That's interesting. What do I call an answer?

Karen I'm happy as I am.

Colin What do I call an answer, Karen?

Karen I don't know.

Colin Is that an answer?

Karen I don't know.

Colin You're happy as you are?

Karen Yes. Yes, I am.

Colin Tell me about your friend.

In your own words. Tell me.

Silence.

Karen I have to go.

She moves away.

Remember the peas.

Colin (What?)

Blackout.

3.3 A ROOM IN THE FEATHERS HOTEL

Liz and Paul.

They kiss.

Paul What's your name?

Liz What's yours?

Paul Paul.

Liz laughs.

Is that funny?

Liz Yes.

76

Paul Why?

Liz It makes me laugh.

Paul You married?

Liz No.

Paul Why does it make you laugh?

Liz Not really.

Paul Not really married.

Liz No.

,

Paul So this is a room. I've never been in a room.

Liz I'm often in a room.

Paul What's your name?

Liz Elizabeth.

Paul Is that your real name?

Liz Doesn't it sound real?

Paul I like that kind of name.

Liz I didn't know I had a kind of name.

,

I've taken you away from your friends.

Paul Who? Gary?

They laugh.

Liz Why don't you have a car?

Paul I don't want any of that.

Liz Any of what?

77

Paul Any of that. I'm not interested.

Liz Can't you drive?

Paul Driving's my job. What's yours?

They laugh.

What's yours?

Liz Driving's your job.

Paul Yes. What's yours?

Liz Manipulating people.

Paul That's nice.

Liz My daughter will tell you my job is manipulating people.

Both faint laugh.

Paul That's nice. How old is she?

Liz How old is Jo?

Paul How old is your daughter?

Liz Why?

Both faint laugh.

My daughter is living on a bus. She's sixteen years old. She's nineteen weeks pregnant.

Distant metallic sound.

Paul Take off your dress.

Liz She lives on the bus, but at weekends she comes home to eat and to wash her hair. That's when I'm told how much she despises me. At weekends I hear how much she despises me. That I should do something useful. That I'm manipulating people. And all this, Paul,

78

with her mouth full of food that I've paid for and put in front of her.

Paul Take off your dress.

Liz I'm the one who's paying.

She takes off her dress, beneath which she wears a full-length slip. Silence.

Paul Are you cold?

Liz No.

Paul Spring is late.

Liz Yes. Is it?

Paul This year spring is late.

Liz I think haven't I heard it's later here?

Paul Perhaps. Perhaps that's what it is.

Liz Perhaps it's colder here.

Paul Are you cold then?

Liz It was cold at the station.

Paul Is that the railway station?

Liz Is there another station?

Paul There's a bus station.

Liz Is that what you drive?

Paul What? A bus? No.

Distant metallic sound.

Liz What is that noise?

Paul STK.

Liz What's STK?

Paul They fragmentise metal.

Liz Even at night.

Paul All night. Scrap. Steel.

Liz How d'you sleep?

She moves away.

You know, Paul, I could tell when I got off the train that this is one of those places where the people are full of energy, they're full of it, but they don't know what to do with it. They've got a railway station and a bus station and a high street with all the big names and they've got a certain level of disposable income which they need to dispose of because just the thought of it is weighing them down. The men are taking their wives round the electrical stores and the wives are taking the men round the clothes stores and the children are following with bags of crisps and it's all because of this thing which is weighing them down. And that's where I come in, Paul. Simply to help them discover exactly what it is that they want. Simply to help them dispose of that thing. Someone – not me – it isn't me – someone – has come up with an idea, they've come up with an idea and all I want to discover is whether it's an idea that appeals to them nowadays. Do they drink coffee? Do they drink it frequently or rarely? Would they put lemon in their tea – and what would that *mean?* What do they feel about a tea-bag with a string? Do you see? So when they come to buy – of their own free will, Paul – come to buy the product and to dispose of that thing then this is a product which they have actively participated in the decision-making process.

Paul moves behind her. He lets down her hair.

Or let's say that I find out, I don't know, that there are

women. Let's say (because there are) that there are women who feel for whatever reason embarrassed about touching themselves. So as a direct result of that, Paul, a product can be produced with an applicator, OK, and it can be targeted at those precise women, for their benefit, for their benefit, Paul, who have those feelings. So all I'm saying is, is what is all this about right and wrong, because that simply does not *apply* here.

Paul presses close behind her. She leans back against him.

Paul Is that true then?

Liz What?

Paul They don't like touching themselves.

Paul puts his left hand between her legs.

Liz So what do you drive?

Paul I'm at Hansford's.

Liz What's that?

Paul Timberyard.

Liz So you deliver.

Paul I drive a fork-lift in the yard.

Liz A fork-lift truck.

Paul A fork-lift.

'

I don't deliver. I'm in the yard.

Liz You move the wood.

Paul I shift timber. Wood is trees.

Distant metallic sound.

Liz So it's manual.

Paul What is?

Liz In the yard.

Paul Very.

Liz Which makes you a D.

Paul What's a D?

Liz (Wood is trees.)

Paul What's a D?

Liz It's how you're grouped, Paul. You're grouped as a D, and your wife is grouped as a D with you.

Paul My wife?

Liz I can feel the ring.

Paul moves his hand, but Liz holds on to his ring finger.

She's wondering where you are.

Paul She's out.

Liz Where?

Paul That's her business.

Liz You trust each other.

Paul breaks away. He takes a can of beer from his jacket pocket and drinks.

Liz Where do the buses go?

Paul Into the villages.

Liz Christ I hate villages.

Paul I hate villages. I was born in a village. It's death.

Liz takes the can and drinks.

When you're fifteen you start going to church-hall discos. You don't really like it. You don't like the noise. But of course you go to the church-hall discos because the girls go and you can drink as much beer as you like out of a paper cup.

Both faint laugh.

So you dance – although it's not really dancing is it – you dance with the girls and if you're lucky you get to walk one of them home in the dark. I mean back to the village. Past the bus shelter.

'

All you want is one thing. (It's death.)

Liz What thing is that?

Both faint laugh.

Paul Can I ask you a question, Elizabeth?

Liz What question?

Paul Why did you upset that man?

Liz What man?

Paul Nigel. Why did you throw that in his face?

Liz He was offensive.

Paul What'd he done to you?

Liz He offended me.

Paul Why did he offend you?

Liz Why don't you ask him?

Paul He's a character, that's all.

Liz (I'm cold.)

83

Paul He's just a character.

Liz I'm cold, Paul. You're right. Let's go out. Take me somewhere.

Paul I don't have a car.

Liz Let's walk.

Paul I like it here. I've never been in a room.

Liz We'll take a taxi.

Paul Where?

Liz Into the country.

Paul It's dark.

Liz Let's go into the country.

Paul It's dark. I don't want the dark, I want to see you.

They kiss.

Liz One little madam tried to wreck my group tonight.

Paul A group of what?

Liz Discussion. A group of women.

Paul What's that?

Liz Because I got through the warm-up fine . . .

Paul What is that?

Liz How many children, husbands . . .

Paul How many husbands . . . (*laughs*)

Liz How many husbands . . . (*laughs*) What commercials they can recall, what hot drinks they use nowadays . . .

Paul Hot drinks . . .

Liz Hot drinks, i.e. these are various kinds of coffee, Paul, chocolate – (*laughs*) Don't make me laugh – and what they use to make these drinks, e.g. do they use water, do they use milk, hot milk, or do they add milk . . .

Paul Don't ask me . . .

Liz I'm not asking you . . .

> *They laugh. Paul becomes more intimate. Liz continues.*

. . . and what times of day do they use these drinks and which drinks do they use at which times of day . . .

Paul (*lifting her slip*) I want to see you.

Liz No. Listen. So we get through that. We're through it. (*More emphatic.*) No. Let me finish. (*She moves away.*) Let me finish, Paul. Because we're through it and OK it's time to introduce them to the concepts, in this case it's a blend, it's a blend of coffee and chocolate.

Paul It's a blend.

Liz That's right. It's a blend, i.e. this is a food product, Paul, not a manifestation of evil. So I'm doing this, I'm introducing the concepts, when Little Miss C2D – whatever she is – pipes up . . .

Paul (*amused*) That's her group.

Liz That's right. C2D women. She pipes up – I can't do the accent – but she pipes up and what she says is, is basically what's going on, what's going on here? She says, what's this about, it's supposed to be about shopping. She says she was told we wanted her views, her opinions. (*With increasing bitterness throughout.*) So I tell her, yes, that's exactly so, I do want her views, but what I want are her views about the product, views about the blend. Not views about the *world*, Paul. Not views about what is or is not *going on here*. Just views about the blend, that's all I want in terms of her views. Because this is not (as I have to point out to her) not a free-for-all. It's not a party. It's not a time to search your soul (either within it or for it). It's not, Christ it's not therapy. It's not a political gathering, Paul, or a charitable body. It's not the Day of Judgement neither is it a game we're playing. It's not any of these things. But nevertheless there's a structure, there are rules, and there is a limit. There is a limit, Paul. Because I have five other ladies in this room, five ladies who are perfectly happy as they are. But this one – to her – I can see it in her eyes that I represent something. What do I represent? I don't know. But whatever it is, it's not something she can deal with. I can't do the accent but if you can imagine someone very short and very pregnant with artificial highlights done in the privacy of her own bathroom, and here she is, it's something she cannot deal with.

,

So I'm calm, Paul. I'm very calm. Little Miss Linda has blue eyes. They're angry but they're also blue and beautiful and they make me calm. I point out that she has been recruited to take part in a group discussion about hot drinks, that there is free wine, that there is a cash gift in an envelope with her name on it. I point out that she has agreed to participate. That she can choose even at this late stage not to participate. But that whatever choice she makes, the effect is the same.

Distant metallic sound. Paul's back is turned.

So what does she do? She walks out. Little Miss Linda walks out. It's a matter 'of principle'.

,

Paul Linda's my wife.

86

Liz I'm sorry?

Paul Linda is my wife.

Liz laughs.

Don't laugh.

Liz I'm not, no . . . (*She laughs.*) I think that's
wonderful. It's tremendous, Paul. It's . . .

,

Paul Don't laugh at her.

Liz I'm not. (*She moves away.*) No. I'm not. Laugh. No.
Of course. No.

She opens her briefcase and takes out an envelope.

Paul What's that? What is that?

Liz Nothing. (It's your . . .) It's just her envelope, her
gift. Take it.

,

Paul What is that?

Liz Just (it's nothing) just take it.

,

Just take it and get out of my room.

Blackout.

3.4 HOME

Liz, Jo, Colin.

*Colin is beating a rhythm on the back of a chair with a
pair of drumsticks. No one speaks. He stops.*

Colin Or someone tells me that I'm made of these things. What are those things I'm supposed to be made of?

Jo Genes?

Colin OK, that I'm made of genes. (Thank you.) And because of these genes I am in some way 'programmed' by some kind of acids . . .

Jo (DNA, RNA . . .)

Colin And these acids are like instructions, is that right?

Jo (Digital instructions.)

Colin OK, so they are instructions (thank you) telling me what I should think, what I should feel, what my needs are. And all that distinguishes me from a machine . . .

Liz I don't think that's true.

Colin Well that's what I'm saying. How can it be?

Colin beats with the sticks. No one speaks. He stops.

Or we're told that the universe – I mean Jesus wept who are these people? – that there is no spirit in the universe but that it consists (am I right?) entirely of particles which are in turn divided . . .

Jo (Sub-atomic particles.)

Colin . . . into sub-atomic (thank you) particles which cannot even be *observed*. Who *are* these people? There they are in Geneva, whatever. Because they can say what they like but I will not be limited in that way.

Jo I'd love to go to Geneva . . .

,

. . . Lake Geneva.

Liz Coffee?

Colin I won't. Thank you. No. My wife is in the car.

Jo Jennifer.

Colin Jennifer – thank you, yes – is in the car.

Liz Won't she come in?

I'll get the tapes.

Liz goes. Colin beats as before. He stops.

Colin How's your friend?

Jo What friend?

Colin resumes beating.

What friend?

Colin (*stops*) Your friend in the field.

Both faint laugh. Colin beats, stops.

I'll tell you something which may please you: I'm thinking of quitting this.

Jo Work?

Colin Drums. I'm thinking of giving up the drums. I'm not sure I'm going anywhere with it. And it's getting on her nerves. Jennifer's a rather nervous person – sensitive – and she'd like me to try something with a melody. This room has been painted.

He beats as before, stops.

What we generally do on a Sunday is we drive around. We don't use a map, we just drive around until we find a pub, this is a country pub, with parking, and that's where we have lunch. (*He beats.*) We like a place with beams, by which I mean real beams that date back to something. (*Beats.*) A low ceiling. In winter a fire. (*Beats.*) What Jennifer likes is a corner seat in the window where we can sit at right angles. (*Beats.*) That way our knees touch. (*Beats.*) I drive there, she drives back. (*Beats.*) On the way back we may talk about the pub. We may compare it with other pubs, other Sundays. (*Beats.*) She has the most wonderful hair.

   Liz enters with tapes.

This room has been painted.

Liz Yes.

Colin White.

Liz Yes.

   Colin slips the drumsticks into a pocket and takes the tapes.

Colin How was the North East?

Liz (What?) Fine, it was fine.

Colin It was OK?

Liz It was (yes) it was fine.

Colin You had a good response.

Liz (Yes.) What?

Colin You had a good / response.

Liz (Sorry.) Yes.

Colin A good sample.

Liz Yes. I lost one.

Colin That happens.

Liz (Yes.) What?

Colin I said, that / happens.

Liz That's right, it happens. (Sorry.)

   Silence.

   Colin snaps his fingers in front of her face.

Yes. I know. Sorry. (*faint laugh*)

Colin I sometimes wonder if you're with us. I sometimes wonder if she's with us, Jo. Are you with us?

Liz Am I what?

   Jo and Colin laugh. Liz joins in.

Colin How is Paul?

Liz Paul?

Colin Yes, I thought he was . . .

Liz What d'you mean: Paul?

Colin (No, I mean, sorry, I thought he was . . .)

Liz Paul.

Colin The writer. I thought he was the writer. Paul.

Liz You mean . . .

Colin Am I wrong?

Liz You mean *Paul*.

Colin Am I wrong? Yes. Paul.

Liz No.

Colin Was it not?

Liz No.

Colin No?

Liz No. You're not. It was.

Colin Well I thought it was.

Liz It was.

Colin That's what I thought.

,

Well, I ought to go.

Liz (I've no idea.)

Colin No idea what? (Sorry . . .)

Liz Where he is. How he is. No idea.

Colin She gets bored, very bored, on her own in the car. And anxious – understandably, I think, anxious.

Jo What about?

Colin About what might happen to her, on her own. Not so much in her own car, funnily enough. But she tends to worry in mine.

Colin puts the tapes away, starts to go.

Well, thanks for this.

Jo (*amused*) What does she think will happen?

Colin Why don't you ask her, Joanna?
See you Monday.

Colin has gone.

Liz Lunch?

Jo Please.

Liz What?

Jo For lunch?

Liz Yes.

Jo Whatever.

Liz Pizza?

Jo Whatever.

,

Yes. Thank you. I'm sorry.

Liz As it is? Or shall I add cheese?

Jo How d'you mean: add cheese?

Liz I sometimes add cheese.

Jo I didn't know that.

,

Shall I do it?

Liz I'll do it.

Jo I don't mind doing it.

,

Really, I don't mind doing it.

Liz Why don't you have a bath?

Jo Do you not mind?

Liz I'll do it. There's nothing to do. You have a bath.

Jo I'd really like a bath.

,

Liz Well go ahead.

Jo What d'you think she's like?

Liz His wife?

Jo What d'you think she's like?

Liz I think she suffers.

They both laugh quietly. Jo stops and puts a hand on her stomach.

Are you alright?

Jo It moved.

Fade.

THE MISANTHROPE

For M

Il n'y a aucune bienveillance
dans l'écriture, plutôt une terreur.

Barthes

Rewriting Molière

For all its formal brilliance, *Le Misanthrope* (1666) is one of Molière's most intensely personal plays. The fierce argument between conformity and nonconformity clearly derives from his experience of the scandals surrounding three plays of the early 1660s – *L'Ecole des Femmes, Le Tartuffe* and *Dom Juan* – where the writer found himself accused of obscenity, and, more dangerously, of atheism. The voices of righteous anger (Alceste) on the one hand and reasonable compromise (Philinte) on the other must have been continually whispering inside his head like good and bad angels as he struggled to come to terms with the ambiguity of his position as both satirist and servant of the cultural and political elite. And it's hard not to see in the play's central relationship – etched in acid – between a middle-aged man and a woman half his age a reference to Molière's own personal life, after his marriage in 1661, aged forty, to Armande Béjart, a young actress of 'vingt ans ou environ'. Equally, it would be a mistake to see Alceste as a self-portrait. The writer remains detached from his character. This is why Alceste, despite the serious overtones, remains a comic creation. In the words of Francine Mallet, 'Alceste is Molière without the irony. Molière knows he looks ridiculous in some situations – Alceste doesn't.'

So how do you 'translate' (literally 'move from one place to another') an artefact that is so much a product of seventeenth-century Paris and Versailles? One answer – and the one I've attempted here – is to opt for a contemporary setting, and then explore the consequences, whatever deviations and departures from the original that may involve. Molière himself was adamant about the actuality of comedy: 'When you portray [tragic] heroes, you can do what you like. They're imaginary portraits, in which we don't expect to recognise ourselves . . . But when you portray real people, you have to paint what you see. The pictures must be accurate. If you don't make *recognisable portraits of the contemporary world*, then nothing's been achieved' (*La Critique de l'Ecole des Femmes*, Scene vi, italics mine). And if, three hundred years later, reflecting the contemporary world has meant taking certain 'liberties' with the text, this is only in the belief that – at this distance in time – reinvention, rewriting of one writer's work by another, is 'fidelity' of the truest and most passionate kind.

On 17 February 1673, Molière, whose health had been deteriorating for some time, coughed up blood during the final scene of *Le Malade Imaginaire,* at the point where the character he played was being 'initiated' as a doctor, in a scathing parody of the medical profession he so abhorred. After the performance he was carried in his chair back to his home in the rue de Richelieu. Two priests refused to come, and a third was too late: he died the same night, aged fifty-one.

His enemies weren't slow to savour the irony. One anonymous poem puts these words into his mouth:

> I performed character-assassinations
> with impunity on kings, the devout, marquis,
>   people of all stations.
> I found the hidden truth behind every character,
> but came to grief playing the part of doctor.
> I died without medical, spiritual or legal aid.
> I played death itself – and with death itself I paid.

A week after Molière's death, on 24 February, his theatre reopened with a production of *Le Misanthrope*.

Martin Crimp
November 1995

For background to Molière's life and work I am indebted to Francine Mallet's Molière *(Paris: Grasset, 1986), from which I have quoted above.*

The Misanthrope in this version was first performed at the Young Vic, London, on 8 February 1996. The cast was as follows:

John William Osborne
Alceste Ken Stott
Covington Niall Buggy
Jennifer Elizabeth McGovern
Ellen Cathryn Bradshaw
Alexander Richard O'Callaghan
Julian Jo Stone-Fewings
Messenger/Simon George Beach
Marcia Linda Marlowe

Directed by Lindsay Posner
Designed by Joanna Parker
Lighting designed by Simon Corder
Original music by Paddy Cunneen
Sound designed by John A. Leonard

Characters

Alceste
a playwright

John
his friend

Covington
a critic

Jennifer
a movie star

Ellen
a journalist

Marcia
a teacher of acting

Julian
an actor

Alexander
an agent

Also required

A Motorbike Messenger
Simon, a musician

All characters are British, except Jennifer,
who is an American.

The time is now, the place is London.

Notes

When a slash (/) appears within the text, this marks
the point of interruption in overlapping dialogue.

Character prefixes have been placed centrally
to conform to the printing practice of Molière's time.

Act One

London.
The principal room of a suite in a luxury hotel.
Doorway to main entrance. Doorway to bedroom.
Alceste bursts through the main entrance, followed
by John.

JOHN

What is it?

ALCESTE

Please leave me alone.

JOHN

What's wrong?
Come on – tell me what the hell's going on.

ALCESTE

Just leave me alone – I'd be eternally fucking grateful.

JOHN

You could at least listen without getting in a state.

ALCESTE

I'll
decide what state to be in, thank you.

JOHN

I just don't understand you.
We're supposed to be friends, then you *pick* on me.

ALCESTE

Friends? Don't make me laugh. Our friendship is
   history.
We used to be friends – OK – correct –

but there are limits to what I'm prepared to accept.
And when I see you talking such total shit
I realise I'm dealing with just one more hypocrite.

JOHN

Alceste, don't tell me you're upset . . .

ALCESTE

Upset? That's the best understatement yet.
To do that to a man with no coercion
is a form of social perversion.
You're suddenly kissing this man on both cheeks:
'Darling – haven't seen you for *weeks* –
if there's anything you need at all
don't hesitate (or was it on his mouth) to call.'
But when I ask you what his game is
you can't even tell me what the bastard's name is.
If I was that compromised, Christ knows,
I think I'd take a fucking overdose.

JOHN (*amused*)

Suicide? Really? But isn't that the quintessent
gesture of the moody adolescent?
Will swallowing fifty paracetamol
really make the world morally more acceptable?

ALCESTE

What's that supposed to be? An example of wit?

JOHN

I'm so pleased you appreciate it.
But come on – for everyone's satisfaction –
tell us your principles of human interaction.

ALCESTE

Never try to deceive,
and only say what you truly believe.

JOHN

But if a man takes me in his arms

106

then I have a duty to say how charmed
I am. If he thinks we relate
then I have a moral duty to reciprocate.

ALCESTE

What total bollocks. Nothing's more effete
than the moral contortions of the self-proclaimed elite.
The slobbering over the ritual greeting,
the bullshit spoken at every meeting
makes me vomit. What kind of morality
makes a fool the equal of a decent man? What kind of
society?
OK, let's say I let myself be assaulted
by one of these people who swear I can't be faulted –
what's the point them eulogising my name
if they treat some cretin exactly the same?
I'm sorry I'm sorry but no one in their right mind
wants (or needs) that kind
of praise. That level of sycophancy
is typical of our moral bankruptcy.
If you value everyone equally highly, I'm afraid you'll
never
have any values whatsoever.
And since you subscribe to the prevailing culture
I dissociate myself from you if as a result you're
keener to lick arses
than make discriminating choices.
I want to be *valued*. I really can't face
people whose embrace
indiscriminately includes the entire human race.

JOHN

But you're part of society – and one of its norms
is to accept the customary forms
of politeness.

ALCESTE

Politeness? I'd introduce extreme penalties
for trafficking in false loyalties.
The purpose (it seems to me) of human discourse
should be to exchange our innermost thoughts
and feelings. In other words what I'm asking
is to see the *man* speaking – not the mask.

JOHN

I can think of places where that philosophy
wouldn't get much sympathy.
Besides – with respect to your ideals –
what's wrong with sometimes hiding what you feel?
Would you really tell certain men and women
exactly what you think of them?
Go up to a fellow artist, say, and start
to tear their precious work apart?

ALCESTE

Absolutely.

JOHN

So you'd really tell the director at this
morning's screening
that the film was anodyne, with no political thrust
or meaning?

ALCESTE

Definitely.

JOHN

And I suppose you'd find that sinister
and point the finger at interference by a government
minister.

ALCESTE

Naturally.

JOHN

You're joking.

ALCESTE

No I'm not.

Not when I've got
so many examples in front of me
of private political and artistic hypocrisy.
I'm enraged. I can't forgive
the way that men and women choose to live.
Everywhere you look: sycophants, compromise, hypocrites,
nepotism, betrayal, vested interests –
I've had enough. Call it insanity
but I take issue with the whole of humanity.

JOHN

I have to say that this so-called rage
would make more sense on the seventeenth-century stage.
And surely as a playwright you're aware
of sounding like something straight out of Molière.

ALCESTE

Jesus Christ, you think you're so clever.

JOHN

You see, you'll never
change society single-handed. And if it's the truth
you're after,
the truth is is that ranting moralists are met by
ridicule and laughter.

ALCESTE

Exactly. That's just what I'd expect.
It would nauseate me to be treated with respect.

JOHN

Are you saying that humanity should be condemned?

ALCESTE

I'm saying that humanity as we know it – yes –
    should come to an end.

JOHN

And are we to take it (because I think you're going
    too far)
that no one is exempt from your *fatwah*?
Is it universal, or will there be some / kind of –

ALCESTE

Universal. I hate everyone.
And not just people in the public eye,
but the public themselves who just stand by
and watch – whose understanding's limited
to absorbing a few selected images.
As you know, I'm in the potentially disastrous position
of allegedly slandering this wretched politician
just by suggesting a 'declaration of his interests'
should include details of his current mistress.
Next thing you know he's posing in his garden
complete with wife, dogs and children
in a grinning parody
of the nuclear family
hoping with the aid of labrador retrievers
to deceive us
into thinking the only people who take lovers
are the poor, the unemployed and single mothers.
And despite this total lack of integrity
he's the one afforded celebrity
status: on the news . . .
interviews . . .
he's free to choose.
While I'm accused
of being malicious and uncouth
when all I've told's the simple truth.
Jesus wept! And you wonder why

I sometimes want to just curl up and die?
I have a dream of a clean white space
entirely disinfected of the human race.

JOHN

Please
could we just ease
up on contemporary morality
and show a little more understanding of human reality.
Wouldn't it be good to see
some flexibility?
(Or even moral relativity?)
After all, society changes,
and there are whole ranges
of valid responses. Extremes are usually dangerous
and often cause unreasonable pain to us.
We live in a complex social matrix:
nothing's solved by getting back to basics.
Perfection's beyond us. Why can't you just go
with the flow?
If you want to castigate society
then please do it well away from me.
I'm as aware as you are of people's malefactions,
they simply don't provoke the same absurd reactions.
I take people as they come. And if someone acts like
    a shit
then – OK – no problem – let's just quietly deal with it.

You know as well as I do the essential rule
is keep calm, stay cool.

ALCESTE

You're so reasonable you make me sick.
You'd stay cool while someone sliced off your prick.
What if a close friend betrays you? Or goes 'n'
has your assets frozen?
What if they sell your story to the gutter press?

Don't you seek redress?

JOHN

Perhaps. Yes.
But I don't lose my temper. It's hard to be 'enraged'
if one is philosophically disengaged.
And the human animal looks far less fearsome
through the prism
of postmodernism.
The world's a mess. Absolutely. We've fucked it.
So why not just sit back and deconstruct it?

ALCESTE

So I should allow myself to come to harm
and stay quite calm?
Words can't express my hatred of corrupt men.

JOHN

Why don't you just shut up then.

Pause.

This court case of yours, how will you influence the
    outcome?

ALCESTE

I shan't. I have implicit trust in the process.

JOHN

So who's going to discredit the principal witness?

ALCESTE

No one. The suggestion's totally / *appalling.*

JOHN

But who's going to photograph the judge kerb-crawling?

ALCESTE

No one. I have justice on my side.

JOHN

That's the legal equivalent of suicide.

ALCESTE

No dirty tricks. The way I see it,
it's an open and / shut case.

JOHN

On your own head be it.

ALCESTE

That's fine.

JOHN

Your litigant's invested
large sums, he has *friends* / who can –

ALCESTE

I'm not interested.

JOHN

Well you should be.

ALCESTE

It's my right to choose.

JOHN

I don't think / that's wise.

ALCESTE

And besides I'm quite happy to lose.

JOHN

You must be / joking.

ALCESTE

Given our sick and twisted judiciary, I trust this
will become a classic example of perversion of the
course of justice.

JOHN

You're out of your mind. This is / *insanity.*

ALCESTE

Losing my case would be a great moral victory.

JOHN

No such thing exists, Alceste. (Really, the stuff you spout
would make intelligent people just fall about.)

ALCESTE

That's their problem.

JOHN

Really? I think it could well
be yours too. But tell
me something: it seems you're not so inflexible
in your attitude to . . . sexual
partners. Not so above it all
you don't notice what's available.
Not so embroiled in your heroic struggle with the
human race
you fail to recognise a pretty face.
I'm just amazed that you should admire
such an unlikely object of desire.
Ellen, I suspect, is secretly rather fascinated by you.
Marcia can hardly disguise the fact that she's
infatuated by you.
But you don't even speak to them any more
since you became obsessed by Jennifer,
a woman whose distaste for monogamy
is already legendary.
And since she's arrived in London
her door's been open to men almost at random.
She flirts, she slags people off. Is that acceptable
just because she's beautiful?
Ever since she crossed the Atlantic
her life in this hotel has been both frivolous and frantic.
Surely she represents everything you most hate?

ALCESTE

She's still very young and vulnerable. Don't underrate

love. I know exactly
what her faults are and in a perverse way they attract
   me.
She takes her success at face value (but then again
that's very American)
and until she gains more insight I'm resigned
(no please don't laugh) to going out of my mind.
My strategy is to let *her* choose
when to reveal her hidden virtues.

JOHN
Hidden is certainly the operative word.
Does she love you?

ALCESTE
           Don't refer
to her like that. Of course she does.

JOHN
So then what's all this fuss
you've been making about her other boyfriends?
   Insecurity?

ALCESTE
Look: all I ask is a one-hundred-per-cent commitment
   to me.
I've simply come here for an explanation,
and to alert her to the seriousness of the situation.

JOHN
Well I'm sorry, but if you ask me,
Ellen would be a far more likely
candidate. It's the kind of opportunity not to be missed:
sex with a radical post-feminist journalist –
reason enough, surely, to try her.

ALCESTE
Reason has no influence over desire.

JOHN

You're beginning to worry me. Any
other man would surely . . .

He sees Covington in the doorway. Slight pause.

COVINGTON

Hello. I'd arranged to meet Jenny
here after the screening
but a message down at the desk said that now this
  evening
is the earliest she can manage. Pity.
But then they told me
(rather begrudgingly)
that you had use of the key.
(Of course that's nothing whatsoever to do with me –
I mean: the key
why should it be?
Obviously.)
But then I thought, well why not take this opportunity
of coming up to see
a man
I've always dreamed of taking by the hand
thereby confirming our friendship
and cementing – dare I say it? Yes I do – a lasting
  relationship.

*He offers his hand to Alceste, who seems unaware of
his existence.*

Excuse me, I thought we were having a conversation.

ALCESTE

Really?

COVINGTON

Or have I misread the situation?

116

ALCESTE

You should just be (I'm not sure) just be aware of the
  danger
of committing yourself to a complete stranger.

COVINGTON

Well I'm sorry if I startled you,
it's just I've always had the very highest regard for you.

ALCESTE

Listen –

COVINGTON

        Of course (yes, don't say it) there are writers
  in more prominent positions,
but none with the breadth, depth and sheer range of
  your dramatic vision.

ALCESTE

Listen –

COVINGTON

        Believe me, this comes straight from the heart
which is why I'm so anxious to start
a genuine friendship – anticipating that any future
benefits will be mutual.
Let's set up a meeting. Where's your diary?
Shall we do lunch?

ALCESTE

        I'm sorry?

COVINGTON

                Is there a problem? Excuse me?

ALCESTE

A problem? No. Hold on. I'm a little overwhelmed –
that's all – to be claimed as a friend
so suddenly . . . I mean without any preliminary . . .

I like there to be a little bit of . . .
(how can I put this?)

COVINGTON
Of mystery?

ALCESTE

Exactly.

COVINGTON
Of course.

ALCESTE
It takes *time* / to make –

COVINGTON
Absolutely.

ALCESTE
– the right choices. I'm afraid I'm (sorry) slightly fanatical
about friendship. (I mean we may be / quite incompatible.)

COVINGTON
Absolutely – you're absolutely right.
Time – yes – a characteristic, if I may say so, insight
into human nature. Brilliant. Meanwhile if there's anything at all
you need (perhaps a little editorial?)
just call
me at the paper.

Produces card.

Or look: phone me at home.
I want you to feel that as an artist you're not alone.
We critics are artists too:
perhaps you don't realise just how much I could do
for you.

118

Who knows – it might even reach the stage
where I could get you on to the front page –
like a Lloyd-Webber musical – or some other natural
    disaster.

Laughs at his own joke.

OK, OK, you're wondering what I'm after:
well the fact is I have something here
(a play actually)
a script I've been working on for the past year –
and I'd love to get your reaction.

ALCESTE (*faint laugh*)
I don't think you'll get much satisfaction
out of me.

COVINGTON
I'm sorry?

ALCESTE
You'll find
I have the unfashionable habit of speaking my mind.

COVINGTON
Exactly. Good. Yes. I don't want you to be nice:
I'm looking for genuine dramaturgical advice –
I mean if there's anything in particular wrong with it . . .

ALCESTE
OK, OK – shall we just get on with it?

COVINGTON
On with it?

ALCESTE
Read it.

COVINGTON
You mean here? Now? In front of you?

ALCESTE

Here. Now. Why not? Wouldn't that be fun to do?

Alceste grins. Covington opens his script and reads.

COVINGTON

'Scene One. Evening. An attic room.' Perhaps I should
 just say
it's more a scene than a complete play.

ALCESTE

OK.

COVINGTON

'A man and a woman' – and it's directly based
on my own personal experience.

ALCESTE

Well that's often the case.

COVINGTON

Exactly. 'Scene One.' Is it? Good. (The man by the
 way is me,
there's a strong element of . . .)

ALCESTE

Autobiography.

COVINGTON

Exactly. Yes. Of course there are more scenes planned.

ALCESTE

Fine. A first draft. I understand.

COVINGTON

'Scene One. Evening. An attic room. A man and a
 woman: Clair.
Clair is young and beautiful.
The man is somewhat older – powerful
but sensitive and aware.'

ALCESTE
(Of what? Sorry? Is this the play?)

COVINGTON
Just aware.

ALCESTE
(Aware. I see. OK.)

COVINGTON
'They look at each other. Silence.'
Pause.

ALCESTE
But what are the characters' intentions?

COVINGTON
Those are just the stage directions.

ALCESTE
(OK. I see.)

JOHN
Two good strong parts.

COVINGTON
Thank you. Now this is where the dialogue starts –

'MAN My darling, let me crush you in my arms.

WOMAN I'm no longer susceptible to your monied charms.

MAN Make love to me. Forget this girlish nonsense.

WOMAN I can't. I have a new-found social conscience.

Pause.'

JOHN
Brilliant. I'm hooked. The theme is timeless.

ALCESTE
(I've never heard anything so completely / mindless.)

COVINGTON

'MAN Remember all the good times that we had.

WOMAN The times that you call good now all seem bad.

MAN Let's dine out at my restaurant. The limousine is
ready.

WOMAN I'd rather stay at home and cook my own
spaghetti.
I'd rather stay at home and find out who I am.

MAN Your name is Clair. And I'm the man
who loves you. Who cares if it's not right!

WOMAN Oh God! Oh God!

They kiss beneath the leaking skylight.'

Closes the script with satisfaction.

There's already interest from the RNT

JOHN
I'm not surprised. I liked the pause particularly.

COVINGTON
You don't think it owes too much to Pinter?

JOHN
Far from it. There's not even a hint of . . .

ALCESTE
(Talent.)

JOHN
. . . plagiarism. In fact I don't think I appear t've
heard anything quite like it in the theatre.
Have you, Alceste?

COVINGTON (*delighted*)
Really?

ALCESTE

(What?)

COVINGTON

D'you mean it?

ALCESTE

(I pity the poor bastards who / have to read it.)

JOHN

Of *course* I mean it. The National's sure to / buy it.

COVINGTON

What d'you think, Alceste? You're being very quiet.

ALCESTE (*smiles*)

Listen. When someone writes a script
it's very hard for them to stand back from it.
I did in fact once read a scene similar to yours
(admittedly without the pause)
but it did give me cause
to wonder what makes people cover page after page
with dialogue so unplayable on the stage.
Why is there so little insight
into the qualities required to be a playwright?

COVINGTON

If you're talking about what I've just read
to you, I / think you should –

ALCESTE

                       That's not what I said.
No. It was more of a rhetorical question.
Listen. Let me make a suggestion:
if someone has zero facility
it's a disability
they should conceal.

COVINGTON

                  Zero facility? Is he talking about me?

ALCESTE

I just said 'someone'. Please don't shout. (You see –
people just have to discuss writing
and they / start fighting.)

COVINGTON

Are you saying I have no talent?

ALCESTE

I'm not saying anything. Perhaps you have – perhaps
    you haven't.
(Although you can still write total shit
and find some fool to workshop it
book a venue for the evening
and subject your friends to a rehearsed reading.)
Whatever. But please – resist the temptation:
you're not going to get an Olivier nomination
(unless of course it's your own).
As a critic you have a certain reputation –
but would you yourself enjoy critical examination?
It's much easier to face a first night
as a critic than a gibbering playwright.

COVINGTON

Yes, but specifically about my scene –
d'you mean / it's –

ALCESTE

Your scene is rubbish.

COVINGTON

                    (Uh-huh. You mean the actual / scene.)

ALCESTE

The way your characters speak is stilted and unnatural.
(The actual scene, yes.)
It's flaccid. The dialogue's weak.
The acid test is to reflect the way that people really
    speak.

'Crush you in my arms'?
'Susceptible to your monied charms'?

COVINGTON
It is a first draft.

ALCESTE
And you wonder why people laughed?
Listen: if you must write a play
it helps not only to have something to say
but also a way of saying it that arrests us
engages us and tests us.
Your dialogue I'm afraid is the verbal equivalent
of industrial effluent
i.e. the tedious platitudes
of emotionally self-indulgent middle-class attitudes –
the kind of waste
that unfortunately we can't legislate against.
(So he loves her, so she's being mean. / Who gives a
    fuck?)

COVINGTON
I'm sorry, but it's a contemporary theme.

ALCESTE
If that's your idea of contemporary
you should be adapting classics for the BBC.
(Being so indifferent to good writing
they'd probably find your work rather exciting.)

John laughs.

No, I'm quite serious:
that kind of sloppy imprecision's
just what they like on television.

COVINGTON
Well I'm sorry, but I've been told it has potential.

ALCESTE

Well of course it's essential
for you to believe that.
(If you didn't want my opinion you / shouldn't've
asked for it.)

COVINGTON

It's already had several rehearsed readings.

ALCESTE

Well naturally – people are afraid of hurting / your
  feelings.

COVINGTON

Well-known actors have read these parts.

ALCESTE

Actors are generous. They have over-kind / hearts.

COVINGTON

Artists are always misunderstood.

ALCESTE

But the hard part is
is the misunderstood are not necessarily artists.

COVINGTON

Well I'd be very interested to see
how you'd handle a similar theme.

ALCESTE

Listen – if I *had* written such a load of crap
I wouldn't be going round advertising the fact.

COVINGTON

I'd advise you not to adopt that tone.

ALCESTE

Oh really? Listen: why don't you just leave me alone.
Go home.

COVINGTON

You're arrogant, rude and totally insensitive.

ALCESTE

And you're becoming increasingly offensive.

JOHN

Please. Both of you. What if she walks in?

COVINGTON

Who? Jennifer? Oh my God have I been
(sorry) shouting? He's right. We'll deal with this (OK?)
another day.

ALCESTE

Absolutely. And thank you so much for showing us
your play.

Covington goes.

JOHN

Congratulations. All he wanted was encouragement
and you turn it into a major incident.
Did you have to make such a big bloody deal of it?

ALCESTE

Just shut the fuck up / will you.

JOHN

                Oh charming.

ALCESTE

                      Hypocrite.

Pause.

JOHN

I hope you realise . . .

ALCESTE

         I'm not listening.

JOHN

Fine.

ALCESTE

Don't interfere.

Pause.

Realise what?

JOHN

Nothing.

ALCESTE

Tell me.

JOHN

Only that you've just ended your career.

ALCESTE

Please. I'm not prepared to discuss the topic.

JOHN

And I'm beginning to find you excessively misanthropic.

Act Two

Alceste, Jennifer.

ALCESTE

Listen: I'm afraid I'm in a mood
today to question your whole incredible attitude.
You're looking at a man at the end of his tether
who's finding it harder and harder to believe we have
   a future together.
Of course I could lie to you,
but that's something I would never do.
I can't say things I don't believe
although it would be far less painful to / deceive you.

JENNIFER

I see. So I've just come back
to listen to – what? – another moral attack?

ALCESTE

Not an attack. Please. I'm talking about your intimacy
with other men – this open-door policy
which – however much I trust you –
my own nature simply can't adjust to.

JENNIFER

Intimacy? Your imagination's hyperactive.
And would you rather I was old and unattractive?
If a man wants to offer me his regards
what do I do? Call in my bodyguards?

ALCESTE

That's not the point. Clearly you will attract men:
the mistake is to actively encourage them.
The kind of signals you emit

give the impression – how shall I put it? –
that you're fair game.
I'm sorry but it's true. I'm not saying I blame
you (please, that's not what I meant)
but to claim your behaviour's innocent
is certainly contentious
(and probably disingenuous).
Perhaps you'd like to explain
for example why again and again
I find Alexander here. I have great difficulty seeing
why you think he's such a wonderful human being.
Unless a stringy grey pony-tail
contributes to your idea of the perfect male.
Or is his liberal use of moisturiser
some kind of greasy sexual appetiser?
I suppose his loft in Covent Garden
is a real come-on.
I hear he's bought some very interesting pieces
involving the use of animal fleeces,
likes girls to wear bobby socks,
and have sex watched by a dead sheep in a glass box.

JENNIFER (*laughing*)

That's *not true*.
For Christsake Alceste, what the hell's gotten into you?
Alex is my agent. He'd sooner read a contract
than attempt high-risk physical contact.

ALCESTE

Then why can't your 'agent' leave you alone?
Why can't he deal with you on the phone?

JENNIFER

You seem to be jealous of the entire male race.

ALCESTE

Well hasn't the entire male race been invited up to this
    place?

JENNIFER

You ought to find that reassuring.
Isn't it just plain boring
to see so many men? Wouldn't it be much more exciting
if there was a favourite I kept on inviting?

ALCESTE

The favourite is supposed to be me.
(And you wonder why I'm going mad / with jealousy.)

JENNIFER

I love you, Alceste. Isn't that enough?

ALCESTE

That's just a word I'm afraid: 'love'.

JENNIFER

Well it's a word I don't use lightly.
(Really I'm not interested in your linguistic / snobbery.)

ALCESTE

Don't use lightly. Please. Come *on*.
You probably say it to everyone.

JENNIFER

Thank you, Alceste. Thank you so much.
Thank you for your kindness, respect and trust.
How charming. But I refuse to be upset.
Let's just say that as far as my love goes, you can forget
it. That way no one can deceive
you but yourself.

ALCESTE

                    Jesus wept, I don't believe
this. I'd like to tear my obsession
out by the roots. Let me confess
something: d'you think I'm remotely pleased
to be in the grip of this disease-
like thing: love? I hate this role:

this humiliating lack of self-esteem and self-control.

JENNIFER
Really? Aren't you used to having feelings?

ALCESTE
Not when it means dealing
with you, no. My love is incandescent.
I won't be treated like an infatuated adolescent.

JENNIFER
I don't understand. Would you rather pick a fight
with me
or spend the night with me?
You say love, but what you seem
to have in mind's a kind of puritanical *régime*.

Phone.

ALCESTE
If you would just – please – stop playing
games, perhaps we could find a way of saying
what we really / feel . . . (Oh Jesus, I give up.)

JENNIFER (*picks up phone*)
Yes? Who is it? Oh, hi! (It's Julian.) No. Come right up.

ALCESTE
I thought you wanted to talk
but no – now some arsehole is going to just walk
in here uninvited. Couldn't it wait? Is it so hard to say
to someone: 'No, come back later'?

JENNIFER
Julian wouldn't appreciate that.

ALCESTE
Julian is a spoilt egotistical overrated showbiz brat.

JENNIFER
Well exactly. He knows so many people

that offending him's a potentially lethal / exercise.

ALCESTE

So now you're going to flatter / his ego by –

JENNIFER

Please. Don't pretend these things don't matter.
I'm frightened he could interfere
with the natural progression of my career
if I start saying no. These people never manage to do
anything useful – but they can damage you.
To make some kind of issue of it would be insane
(and besides he supplies me with cocaine).

Phone.

ALCESTE

Yes yes yes. Always some excuse not to be alone
with me. And now – Jesus Christ – it's the phone
again. There's absolutely no / *privacy*. I thought we'd
  agreed.

JENNIFER (*picks up phone*)

Oh hi! Alexander. How *are* you? Come right up.

ALCESTE (*makes to go*)

Alexander. That's all I need.

JENNIFER

Where're you going?

ALCESTE

Out.

JENNIFER

Please stay.

ALCESTE

And be humiliated?

133

JENNIFER

But Alceste.

ALCESTE

No.

JENNIFER

Please.

ALCESTE

I'm sorry but I'm not affiliated
to this particular club.

JENNIFER

But just for today.

ALCESTE

You're being absurd.

JENNIFER

How? By asking you to stay?
Why? Is it so unreasonable to request
just a modicum maybe of graciousness?

ALCESTE

Sit there, you mean, and listen to their trivia.

JENNIFER

Please. For me.

ALCESTE

I've said no.

JENNIFER

Just go then if you're so fucking superior.

*They realise that Julian and Alexander along with
John and Ellen have appeared and witnessed the end
of the argument. Brief silence.*

ELLEN

We met this pair in the elevator.

JENNIFER

Ellen. How *are* you?

They kiss.

ELLEN

Are we still OK for the interview?

JENNIFER

Absolutely. Looking forward to it.
Julian. Alex. Hi! Can I put you two on hold for just
a minute?

She takes Alceste aside.

So. Are you staying?

ALCESTE

Only if you stop this degrading game-playing.

JENNIFER

Please shut up.

ALCESTE

Then state your position.

JENNIFER

You're being embarrassing.

ALCESTE

Then make a decision.

JENNIFER

A *what*?

ALCESTE

Yes. Them or me.

JENNIFER

You are joking.

ALCESTE

Not at all. You forget I'm not frightened of provoking /
your pet celebrities.

Alceste moves away as Alex comes up and kisses Jennifer.

ALEX

Well fuck and fuck again. I've just fucked up a crucial
    deal
by offending Tony at the end of our meal.
I automatically offered him a cigarette
and he interpreted this as a personal – and I'm
    absolutely serious – death-threat.

JENNIFER

That's so typical. Tony's an object-lesson in narcissistic
    self-obsession.
And since the move to LA, he's become a born-again
non-smoking spa-drinking low-fat high-jog safe-sex
    Californian.

JULIAN

Talking of self-obsession, I've just spent the last
hour on the phone with Debbie in tears. She just
can't come to terms with the plain
fact that her career is over. But what can you say?

JENNIFER

Julian – you're too kind-hearted.
From what I hear it never even started.
The woman's thirty-two and yet
she's still waiting to be offered Juliet.

JULIAN (*laughs*)

(Oh you bitch.)

JENNIFER

(She *told* me.)

ELLEN (*switches on her tape machine*)
Is it OK to quote you on that?

JENNIFER

I'm sorry? Quote what you like, Ellen. It's a fact.

Laughter.

ELLEN

Have you enjoyed working with Philip?

JENNIFER

Yes. I think it was an OK relationship.
Phil's quite authoritarian on the set
but still gives you the space to let
yourself be creative. It's just hard not to despise
a man who's always undressing you with his eyes.
I'm immune. But I do pity those young women
who are prepared to play along with him.
So. Yes. I respect his work –
but in personal terms the man's a total jerk-off.

Laughter.

ELLEN

What about Jeanette?

JENNIFER

What can I say?
Jeanette is one of the bravest women working in the
    business today.
At least that's what I read
in all your papers – about how she's succeeded
in giving a voice to whatever – to minorities.
But I have it on good authority
that she's intensely homophobic – and never happier
than when she's attacking the so-called 'gay mafia'.

ELLEN

Can you comment on her relationship with Leavis?

JENNIFER

Comment? I could write you an entire thesis.

Now there's a writer with no imagination
who's still managed to carve out a reputation
for being at the cutting edge
despite having no feeling for form or language.
He gets a team of actors, the backing of some institution
then goes off to 'workshop' a revolution.
The political complexities
of several centuries
are thoroughly investigated for about ten days –
whereupon he flies back home and writes another of
  his dreadful plays.
He patronises a nation's plight
while the critics praise his compassion and insight.
(I mean is this work political
or just plain parasitical?)

Laughter.

ELLEN
Have you met Morris?

JENNIFER
  Abominable.
He thinks of himself as the Delphic fucking oracle.
He delivers diatribes against the state
from the comfort of his mansion in Notting Hill Gate.
And his righteous indignation
is matched only by the size of his personal fortune.

Laughter.

ELLEN
How about Clair? Have you been?
I know people rave about her cuisine.

JENNIFER
That's right: she collects exotic recipes
and is rightly famous for her dinner parties.

ALEX

Her flambéed *escalopes* are truly amazing.

JENNIFER

If only her intellect were equally blazing.
The most interesting subject simply sparks
off a string of totally banal remarks.

Laughter.

ELLEN

I believe you know Simon.

JENNIFER

Yes. Why? Simon is a personal friend of mine.

JOHN

I've heard he's extremely bright.

JENNIFER

So bright he'll spend half the night
proving it. Do you *believe* a man
who speaks entirely in epigrams.
Poor Simon. He can't relax. He's ineffectual
because his responses are purely intellectual.
I doubt that he could make *love* to me
without supplying a critical commentary
with footnotes. And when he's taken coke
he starts to babble on about the *baroque*
and how it would've been such ecstasy
to've lived in a previous century
and all that shit. How nothing written today
compares to the music of Lully or Marin Marais
blah blah blah. Which is when of course he starts to
    fumble at my dress
– and promptly loses consciousness.

Laughter.

JULIAN (*with admiration*)
That's Simon so exactly. *God* she's a bitch.

ALEX
What you have there, Jenny, is a very special gift.

ALCESTE
That's it. Go on. I notice your attacks
are only made behind people's backs.
If those people walked into this room
now you'd soon
be all over them with darling this
and darling fucking that.

ALEX
Don't accuse us of hypocrisy:
speak to our resident celebrity.

ALCESTE
But it's you and your entourage
who encourage
her. It's your pseudo-conviviality
that feeds her taste for this point-scoring triviality.
She might be less sarcastic
if she was deprived of her enthusiastic
audience. Flattery
destroys an individual's critical faculty.

JOHN
But doesn't this all sound rather familiar?
Aren't your pet hates actually rather similar?

JENNIFER
Yes, but contradiction is
this man's *vocation*. His
reputation is such that he'd
lose face if he was seen to agree
with anyone – let alone me.
He's so in love with the idea of a fight

that the left half of his brain is at odds with the right.
And if someone *else* expresses an opinion he shares,
   then that's it:
he attacks it.

Laughter.

ALCESTE

Yes, yes – very funny. But then in this company I'd be
   surprised
not to find myself satirised.

JOHN

But come on: admit
you're genetically predisposed to contradict.
It's a sickness. He gets equally mad
if you call something good or the same thing bad.

ALCESTE

That's because people are always wrong.
The sickness is they've no idea what's really going on.
Their critical criteria are rubbish. All
their judgements are entirely superficial.

JENNIFER

Oh, *please* . . .

ALCESTE

Please what? Don't you realise
you're just an amusing object in these men's eyes?
OK. It's very entertaining. But you should try
asking what they say about you in private.

ALEX (*smoothly*)

Listen: it would be neither professional nor gallant –
he's lying, darling – for me to rubbish my own best
   client.

JULIAN

What can I say?

You know we all love you. You're a babe.

ALCESTE

Don't you see they're just bullshitting you?
I may be upsetting you
but at least that's a function of my sincerity.
I hate to see
you living at this skin-deep level
never taking the time or trouble
to question what your life's really about.
I mean why can't you just throw these people *out*?

JENNIFER (*upset*)

Sincerity? Don't you just mean
you want to make an unpleasant scene?
Your programme of instruction apparently depends
on insulting both myself and my closest friends.

To Ellen.

Are you still taping this?

ELLEN

If you don't mind. I think it's shaping
into a very interesting piece,
and it's the unguarded moments like these
that are so revealing
about what my subjects are really experiencing and
    feeling.
If I didn't believe you were the new female icon
I wouldn't've dared to leave the mic on –
but you see I find your sexual politics
fascinating. It seems the trick is
to surround yourself with men
and yet have no specific psychosexual need for them.
Am I right? And of course you don't have to answer me
but I also get this so so weird seventeenth-century
feel from all of this. It's like I'm in a room of stock

characters. It's not postmodern, it's *baroque*.
It's quite unsettling, but then again
perhaps this is the style of the new millennium:
a pre-enlightenment sense of linguistic formality
coupled with post-post-industrial virtual reality.

Everyone looks at her.

(. . . Or something like that.)

ALCESTE
Well if you want my opinion . . .

JENNIFER
Haven't we already had it?

ALCESTE
I beg your pardon?

JENNIFER
Would anyone like to see the wonderful roof garden?

To Alex and Julian.

What, are you leaving?

JULIAN
Are we?

ALEX
Of course not.

ALCESTE (*to Jennifer*)
That would put you in something of a spot
wouldn't it. It would mean you were free
to speak to me.

JULIAN
I've got nothing till this afternoon.
What about you? Are you going soon?

ALEX

Me? I don't need to get away
until our office opens in LA.

JULIAN

(When's that?)

ALEX

(Four p.m. our time.)

Phone.

JENNIFER (*over previous two lines*)
Why are you behaving like this?

ALCESTE

I'm just trying to test your priorities.

JENNIFER (*picks up phone*)
Yes? Hello? I see. So he's on his way.
OK.
It seems there's a young man in a leather jacket
coming up to deliver an urgent packet
to Alceste.

ALCESTE

I don't think that's at all likely.

JENNIFER

But he asked for you at the desk – one of these . . .
    motorcycle
people . . .

ELLEN

Courier.

JENNIFER

Courier. Thank you.

The Messenger appears – long hair, beard, leathers.

Oh my

he's here already. (*to Alceste*) Now just try
and be nice to him.

MESSENGER
Package for Alceste.

ALEX
Please. Come in.

MESSENGER
If you could just sign here and print your name before
you take . . .

ALCESTE (*doing so*)
OK, OK. Are you sure this isn't a mistake?

*He signs and takes the 'package' – a letter – to one
side, opens it and reads. Jennifer meanwhile intercepts
the Messenger.*

JENNIFER
Don't you get hot in all that leather?

MESSENGER
Depends. Y'know. On the weather.

ALCESTE
Jesus wept.

JULIAN
Bad news?

ALCESTE
I don't believe it.

To John.

Just look at that. The bastard. Take it. Read it.

John takes the letter.

JENNIFER (*takes Messenger's arm*)
What is this? You're upsetting our visitor.

JOHN (*faint laugh*)
I don't understand. It's from Covington's solicitor.
He's threatening to sue for defamation . . .

JENNIFER
Have I missed something?

JOHN
        . . . unless he gets a full retraction
of the quote 'malicious attack' unquote on his play
in progress.

ALCESTE
     He's not going to get away
with this.

JOHN
     He claims to be suffering mental distress
and loss of earnings as a direct consequence.

JENNIFER
You mean Covington the *critic?*
That's ridic-
ulous.

JOHN
Nevertheless it might be sensible to compromise.

ALCESTE
What? You want me to tell lies?
I'm going to fight.
This is a man who destroys writers' reputations
   overnight.
Mental distress? No way will I praise
his crappy little stabs at writing so-called plays.

JOHN
I still think you should / calm down.

MESSENGER
          Uh . . . Is there a reply?

ALCESTE

Yes there is. Tell him I'd rather die
than retract. And you can pass on
the message that his reviews aren't fit to wipe my
    arse on.

To Alex and Julian, who are trying not to laugh.

And perhaps you two would like to explain
just what you both find so / entertaining.

MESSENGER

So. OK. Shall I wait while you / write that down?

ALCESTE (*to Jennifer*)

And don't think I've forgot-
ten our previous conversation. (*to Messenger*) What?

MESSENGER

I said: shall I wait while you write that down?

ALCESTE

No. You can find another helmet and bike me into
    town.

Act Three

Alexander, Julian.

ALEX
You always look so unconcerned.
I wish I could've learned
to be like you. I'm fascinated. You seem blessed
with perfect equanimity. Don't you ever get depressed?

JULIAN
What about?

ALEX
(Because I do.)

JULIAN
There's no secret:
what you see, Alex, is what you get.
Mummy's famous – so is Dad. Of course I've taken
some trouble
to get noticed – but it's hardly been a struggle.
The transition from teenage idol
to stage and film was painless, so I think I'm entitled
to feel fairly pleased with myself:
I've got work, women, prestige, *ridiculous* (at my age)
wealth.
I've experimented with guilt, but I'm afraid self-doubt
just doesn't suit me. I'm bright, I'm talked about,
and I have got talent
(and I could name others in my position who haven't).
Basically what it means
is I've inherited all the useful genes
get all the attention in my scenes

and feature regularly in the Sunday magazines.
Worrying about what to wear is the closest
I ever come to what might be called neurosis.
Oh – and my teeth: if I do have a failing
it's my obsession with a three-monthly clean and
    descaling.
But depression? You're joking. I wouldn't want to be
anything other than what I am. (I have no problems
    mentally.)

ALEX

Nevertheless you appear
to be wasting your time here.

JULIAN

D'you really think so? No, I don't invest
my energy unless I'm confident of success.
I'm not one of these pathetic men
who thoroughly degrade themselves when
it comes to women. Anguish
and so on is not my style. The language
of love – let's face it –
is really pretty bloody basic.
I'm making an investment here and expect to earn
a very comfortable return.
I gamble – of course – but I always win:
I always take out more than I put in
(if you get my meaning) – and the clincher
is: to sleep with me would be something of a coup for
    her.
But what about you? I bet you're
after her yourself, you old lecher.

ALEX

I take a purely paternal interest.

JULIAN

Oh yes? And does that extend to incest?

Both laugh.

ALEX

OK. But I still think you're being rather blinkered.
I'd advise you to think hard
about this.

JULIAN

Blinkered? Oh, absolutely.

ALEX

Jennifer's – listen – very astute. She
gives nothing away – unless she's said . . .

JULIAN

What?

ALEX

. . . something to you. Has she?

JULIAN

Only 'come to bed'.

ALEX

Bullshit.

JULIAN

Well that was the implication.

ALEX

Implication bullshit. It's all in your imagination.
No – are you *serious*?

JULIAN

I'm as serious as you are.

ALEX

Stop. Listen. This isn't getting either of us very far.
Are you fucking her – or not?

Pause.

JULIAN

Not.

ALEX

OK.

JULIAN

Lunch is as far as I've got –
even then she turned up late
and spent the whole hour pushing steamed broccoli
round her plate.

ALEX

Then listen: you're a betting man
aren't you. Yes? OK, then here's the plan:
prove to me you've had her – your word is sufficient –
and I'll waive my next six months' commission.
But, if you're the loser
and I seduce her,
then I pay my next six months' rent
by taking an additional ten per cent.
Do we have an agreement?

JULIAN

But that's obscene. How can you put such a disgusting
take on it?
I couldn't. No. (*lowers voice*) She's coming. OK.
Quick, let's shake on it.

They shake hands as Jennifer enters.

Hi.

JENNIFER

So. What are you two up to?

ALEX

Oh. Nothing.

JENNIFER

Is that why Julian's blushing?

Pause. Phone.

Excuse me.

JULIAN (*sotto voce*)
Have I gone really red?

ALEX (*sotto voce*)

Idiot.

JENNIFER (*picks up phone*)
Hello? Well stop her. Say I'm sick in bed
or something. OK, OK, I realise it's not your fault.

ALEX

Is there a problem?

JENNIFER
It seems that Marcia's called
and is on her way up here. I gave express
instructions she wasn't to get past the front desk.

JULIAN

I'm out of here. That woman's unbearable.
Alex, are you coming?

JENNIFER
That's not very charitable.
Surely you're not leaving when
you know how much she enjoys the company of
    bright young men?
She probably knows you're here –
how's she going to feel if you just up and disappear?
No wonder she's incredibly bitter
if this is the way you're going to treat her.
This is a woman who's lonely and damaged,
who's never even managed
to keep a partner. She needs therapy

but hides instead behind an ideology
of outmoded feminist
rhetoric.
And because Alceste once kissed
her (they were both drunk) at an opening night
party, she now thinks she has some kind of right
over him – which is basically why she hates me
and tries to stir up serious shit against me.
I used to respect her as a teacher – but there's a glitch –
she's become a totally intolerable malicious . . .

Marcia appears.

                                          . . . which
way did you come up? Security
only just this minute got in touch with me.

They kiss.

MARCIA
The stairs, darling. I'm trying to take more exercise.

JENNIFER
But this is such a wonderful surprise!

MARCIA (*to the men*)
Pleased to meet you.

But the men slip out.

                        Don't they believe in protocol?

JENNIFER
Drink?

MARCIA
        No thank you. You know I never touch alcohol.

Jennifer pours herself a big drink.

Jenny, I've always (as you know) had a great deal of
    respect for you

153

which is why I'm not afraid to be direct with you
about your work. When I taught you at Juilliard
you were the star student. It wasn't hard
to predict your success. But what really struck
    everybody
was your fantastic integrity.
But since this last film's come out, there are influential
    (as I'm sure you know) voices
highly critical of your artistic choices,
and I've learned
enough to be really rather deeply concerned.
People are saying (and if you knew how much it hurts
    me)
that what you're doing is just one step from
    pornography.
Yes. They're saying you're an artistic coward
to consistently play women who are disempowered
or psychotic.
Of course I pointed out that what you're doing is
    erotic
not exploitative. But I sensed
they weren't too convinced by that defence.
And although I far from agreed
I did (under the most enormous pressure) have to
    concede
that your image on the screen
may be (possibly) undermining women's self-esteem,
that they have a right (yes) to be disappointed
if you even *appear* to be exploited,
that your style of living
(I mean look at it)
is not an appropriate model for today's women.
Listen: I'm not saying you've sold out,
I'm just saying I'm worried about
you. You're not corrupt, but be aware that you're
entering a morally grey area.

I know that you're sufficiently intelligent
to realise that this advice is well meant.
And I wouldn't've even mentioned it
if I didn't feel we had a very special relationship.

JENNIFER

Well thank you, Marcia. You've given me a great deal
to think about. And I feel
that far from taking offence (as one might) at what
　　you say,
I'd prefer to instantly return the favour.
And since you've shown such great integrity
by repeating what's said about me,
the very least that I can do
is repeat (much as it pains me) what people say about
　　you.
I threw a party here the other night for intellectuals
(including I may say radical homosexuals
of both camps). And I hope I'm not betraying
　　anyone's trust
to say that you were discussed.
People said that your attitude to (so-called) pornography
would be funny
if it wasn't so deeply reactionary.
They attributed your need to criticise and interfere
to the exemplary mediocrity (I think that was the
　　phrase) of your own career
and suggested that jealousy
and confused sexuality
might be at the root of what they called the banality
of your opinions. *Professionally* you were accused of
　　muscling in
on actors' work (like Lee Strasberg did to Marilyn)
– trying to maintain a niche
for the discredited techniques you teach.
It was so distressing to hear you abused –

particularly when the word 'dinosaur' was used.
Someone suggested (surely in error)
that the scenes you condemn in the movies are the ones
    you'd like to see in your own bedroom mirror.
They even mentioned your lack of prudence
in attempting to seduce your more vulnerable students,
and could only imagine that this must be
the what? – the legacy of Stanislavksi?
Naturally I leapt to your defence
and tried to prevent this (my God it was *intense*)
onslaught from developing. But I was a lone
voice. (And the tone
was far from friendly,
believe me.)
They felt that you lacked insight
and acted principally out of spite.
They claimed your long-standing grudge meant
you were disqualified from objective judgement.
So maybe it would be (don't you think) wise
to be a little less quick in future to criticise?
I *think* that you're sufficiently intelligent to realise
that this advice is well meant.
And I wouldn't've even mentioned it
if I didn't feel we had a very special relationship.

MARCIA

Of course I expected
insults, but not to be subjected
to this. I'm all the more disturbed,
Jennifer, because I've so obviously touched a nerve.

JENNIFER

Oh really? No, I think we should start
to have these heart-to-hearts
more regularly. Far from being frightening
I find it very very enlightening.
Let's make a deal:

how would you feel
if we agreed
to always report what's said about you and what's
    said about me?

MARCIA

What? Act as your private detective
in return for more lies and invective?

JENNIFER

You see, I'm sure the moral values we apply
undergo subtle changes as the years roll by.
And what one person sees as a celebration
of the body, another sees as cynical exploitation.
Perhaps the work I do now will seem outrageous
when I've reached middle age as
you've done, and have a chance to reassess.
I do appreciate your maternal interest:
but life must be pretty empty
if you're not allowed to be wild at twenty.

MARCIA

Age is irrelevant. This society
is a male-led *as you well know* capitalist conspiracy
which undervalues woman's function
except as teenage objects for immediate sexual
    consumption
on every poster and magazine cover.
Besides, what makes you think I'm old enough to be
    your mother?

JENNIFER

What makes *you* think you have a right
to even be here? As it is I'm being polite,
but I could pick up that phone
and have you thrown
out. Yes. Don't you see: you are totally alone.

Pause.

I am the complete focus of all attention.
And if for reasons too . . . unbearable to mention
you can't handle it, I'm sorry. But the media's
fascination with me isn't my fault. They need an
icon. You heard her say it. And as for my body,
I intend to remain its sole authority.
If your own is subject to the influence of time,
then that's your problem, I'm afraid, not mine.

MARCIA
I never thought I'd live to see the day
Jennifer when you could talk that way
about a friend. Throw me out?
Listen young lady, it's about
time you confronted one or two home truths
about your career. I'm afraid you stand to lose
not just your integrity
and your dignity
but also any vestige of personal privacy.
Who's really in control? Can't you see you've been
sucked into the publicity machine
and spat out as pure product?
Are you really so completely mind-fucked
as to think there's some connection between your
    fame and your own ability?
No, you're just a brand of femininity
to be sold. Your face
is just one more image in the market-place,
and your body
is pure commodity.
Stars aren't born, my darling, they're made
in the world of capital and trade.
The question's not whether your name's up in lights,
the question is: who owns the rights?

JENNIFER
But if it's so easy to become a star
then how very strange it is that you are
a what? A nobody?

MARCIA
Careful,
or I shall be forced to descend to your level.

Alceste enters, unseen by the two women.

Oh I know I'm not welcome here
and you'd prefer me – like your conscience – to just
   disappear.

JENNIFER (*sees Alceste*)
Not welcome? But it's been delightful.
You are a true friend. Alceste, she's so insightful
and what I particularly admire
is that very special wisdom you can only acquire
with age.

*She puts her arms around them both and leads them
downstage.*

Listen, do promise me you'll both be wearing
the wonderful costumes I've been preparing
for this evening's little party. The theme's Louis
   Quatorze –
the kind of thing an American in Europe just adores.

Pause.

Look, why don't I leave the two of you to have a talk.
It's one o'clock. I promised I'd call my parents in New
   York.

Jennifer goes into the bedroom. Silence.

MARCIA (*faint laugh*)
Louis Quatorze?

In the old days this would be the scene where I wait
   for my carriage
while we discuss things like 'love' and 'marriage'.

Pause.

I can't tell you how much your work means
to me. You write the kinds of scenes
that mysteriously reveal the human
condition. And particularly as a woman
I feel drawn to you. I only wish
your work was better known. Rubbish
gets all the attention. You ought to be a household
   name.

ALCESTE

I like to think I have a modicum of fame.
And for the moment
at least, it's proportional to my actual achievement.

MARCIA

But you're much too modest. People get famous
for achieving far less.
A real artist like yourself may not know how to seize
the relevant opportunities
which I / might be able –

ALCESTE

                Please God, don't let's start
a conversation about what is or is not art.
Besides, what major institution
isn't in a state of abject aesthetic confusion?

MARCIA

Yes, but true art makes its own conditions.
I know people in powerful positions
who speak very highly of you –
no – really – they do.

ALCESTE

People will speak highly of a pile of shit
if they've dressed up and spent fifty quid to see it.
I mean could you really bear
to sit through another play by Stoppard or by David
    fucking Hare?
Or watch an audience gratefully reacting
to yet another *tour de force* of classic over-acting?

(*C'est un scélérat qui parle.*)

MARCIA

Be careful who you attack.
(Is it legal to use real people's names like that?)
No, you'd be surprised
at who I know. Without being at all compromised
you're welcome to use
my connections in any way you choose.

ALCESTE

I'm afraid what you're
suggesting is anathema.
I just haven't been designed
to get down on my knees and lick unwiped behinds.

Marcia makes a face.

You see: if what I say disgusts
you then how could you possibly trust
me with your friends. When I select an epithet
I'm not concerned with things like etiquette.
My chronic inability to dissimulate
means I'm fated
to be excluded from the centres of power
with all the advantages they can confer.
So – yes – I break the rules,
but at least I don't have to suffer the company of fools.

MARCIA

Yes. Well. I see it's a sensitive subject.
What interests me more is what exactly is the object
of your visits here? I assume you're not . . .
 emotionally
involved? If so you've no notion
of what you're dealing with. A man with your panache
deserves better than a piece of transatlantic trash.

ALCESTE

That's an extraordinary thing to say
about someone you claim
as a friend.

MARCIA

 Perhaps. Only I'm concerned
you're going to get your fingers very badly burned.
It hurts me to see you so obsessed
when you're not (as you probably know) her principal
 interest.

ALCESTE

What's that supposed to mean?
What exactly has she been / saying to you?

MARCIA

She may be my friend, but that doesn't make her
yours, darling. She's all on the surface. Don't take her
at face value.

ALCESTE

I refuse to believe she's intrinsically shallow:
my mind's made up – and however strange it
seems to you, nothing will change it.

MARCIA

Fair enough. I'll draw my own conclusions
then and leave you to your romantic illusions.

ALCESTE

Come back. No. Marcia.
Wait. What can you do to substantiate
your accusations? You can't plant the seeds of doubt
like that and just walk out.

MARCIA

Can't I?

Pause.

Alright. Then step this way
and I'll show you my exhibit A.
Come back to my flat with me
and you'll find out everything you ever needed to
   know about infidelity
(hers I mean) but were afraid to ask.
Come on. The world's not going to fall apart.
But if it does I'll offer you what consolation
I can by way of compensation.

Act Four

Ellen, John.

JOHN

It was the most incredible sight:
he jumps off the motorbike – right? –
and immediately starts hammering on Covington's
    door.
Covington appears in shock at the first-floor
window and tells him to fuck off or he'll call the police
(I'm parked at the end of the street just in case).
Alceste says, 'You told me to call you at home
you bastard, and here I am.' 'I'm phoning
them now,' says Covington. Slams the window shut.
    Silence.
There's this feeling of potential violence.
Then the door opens: Covington grins
(a new tactic) says, 'Listen, why don't you come in
and discuss this.' (Although the door's still on the
    chain.)
'No,' says Alceste. 'I'll say what I have to say
out here. I've nothing against you as a man
or as a journalist – I've even been a fan
of yours in that capacity –
but please have the sagacity
to see that writing reviews is a world apart
from writing plays – which is: Art.
I gave you my sincere opinion, and issuing a writ
against me isn't going to alter it.'
Well Covington looks as if he's going to burst
into tears. Perhaps that's why Alceste

becomes amazingly (for him) polite.
'Let's shake hands,' he says. 'It's not dignified
to turn this into a vendetta.
After all, your play does have almost infinite potential
  to be better.'

Ellen laughs.

Poor Covington can't argue any more, but
quickly shakes his hand and clicks the door shut.

ELLEN

He certainly knows how to create a scene.
It's almost touching – d'you know what I mean? –
for a man still to believe that words like 'dignified'
are not just signs, that what is signified
by 'love' or 'sincerely'
can exist independently of literary theory.

JOHN

Yes, and he's particularly Quixotic
in the way he sentimentalises the erotic.
His attitude to gender shows no respect
for any of the more important texts.
He still treats Jenny
as if she was his own personal property.

ELLEN

I know. It's shocking.
I sometimes wonder if he's mocking
us: seeing just how far he can go
with a perfect simulacrum of machismo.

JOHN

D'you think she believes in 'love' as such?

ELLEN

Jenny? I don't think she 'believes' in much
at all. She's far too intelligent
not to question –

but at the same time far too confused
to see the subtle ways in which she's being abused.

JOHN

It worries me to see *him* drawn in
to this situation. I've tried to warn him
off. I even suggested – just as an experiment –
that he might well benefit –
I suppose as a kind of re-education –
from having a relationship
with you.

ELLEN (*amused*)
            Really? Do you always recommend me
then for sexual therapy?
Listen: what the two of them get up to
is their business. Yes, I'd love to
see them both happy at least
(although I am in the process of publishing a piece
which suggests that's unlikely). But as
for offering myself as a consolation prize,
experimentally or otherwise,
I'm not
sure that I've got
the nerve to be that pro-active
(nor, I have to say, do I find him remotely attractive).

JOHN

Well just be warned. In his present
state of mind he's likely to resent
any hint of rejection. And to me
you look like perfect material for his next obsessive
    fantasy.
Of course things may still work out between them
in which case we may even see them
an item yet. And if they do become a pair
then assuming you're not involved elsewhere
and can commit to it intellectually,

perhaps the two of us could . . .

ELLEN (*amused*)
       Could *what*? Are you coming on to me?

JOHN
Now that's a question
I'd rather was answered by a semiotician.
To do it justice we'd really need to start
a dialogue with Derrida or Roland Barthes.

*They're both laughing as Alceste enters in intense but
suppressed rage.*

ALCESTE
Where is she?
How dare she
humiliate me.

ELLEN
It's not the end of the world already?

ALCESTE
The end of the world would be
preferable . . . I'm going to do something violent
in a moment.
Where the hell is she? (I can't even *think* / straight.)

ELLEN
I'm afraid she's not here. Calm down.
                 Get him a drink for / Godsake.

ALCESTE
How can someone so beautiful
have no sense at all of what is moral?

ELLEN
What? Is there a / connection?

ALCESTE
                 It's a total inversion
of values. It's disgusting. It's perversion.

Jennifer. After all the assurances she gave me . . .
Jennifer. Jennifer. Jennifer has betrayed me.

ELLEN

Isn't this all rather possessive?

JOHN (*hands Alceste a drink*)
Please don't be so aggressive.
Come on now. Perversion? What is this?

ALCESTE

Why don't you just mind your own fucking business.

Gulps the drink.

I've just been given a tape on which is her own
      profession
of guilt – a confession
(if you can possibly imagine a woman loving him)
of her relationship – yes – with Covington.
The man I thought she found so numbingly boring
turns out to be chief client of her compulsive whoring.

JOHN

Using that kind of language
can only exacerbate – don't you see – the damage.

ALCESTE

Don't tell me Mr Self-Abuse
the words I can or cannot use.

ELLEN

But he's right. This vocabulary is problematic.

ALCESTE

OK then. Let's stop talking and get pragmatic.
If she's capable of gross betrayal
and all the pain that entails,
I'm prepared to reciprocate –
assuming it's not too late
that is to take up your offer.

ELLEN (*glancing at John*)
Offer? I'm sorry?

ALCESTE
To become my lover.
John's right. A calculated gesture
like that will really test her
nerve. When she sees me transfer my attention
onto you she'll regret ever seeing that unmentionable
    little man.
Sweet revenge. You're right. It's the perfect plan.

A slight pause as Alceste pours himself another drink.
He continues to drink heavily throughout this act.

ELLEN
Listen . . . I realise you're upset. But that said
(and maybe the drink's gone to your head
or whatever) I'm not aware of any such 'plan'.
Unless John (what exactly have you been saying?) can
perhaps elucidate?
(Thank you so much, John.) But at any rate
surely this so-called 'love' of yours
should make you blind to whatever flaws
she may have. Isn't that what every cliché teaches us
from Marcel Proust back to Lucretius?

ALCESTE
There's no question of forgiving her.
This is life, not literature.
I intend to make
a complete break.

He drinks, self-absorbed, and doesn't notice that
Jennifer is in the room looking questioningly at Ellen
and John.

ELLEN (*quietly amused, to Jennifer*)
Things seem to be more than he can bear.

JOHN

Come on. Let's see what we're going to wear.

As they go out.

Look, I'm so sorry if I embarrassed you . . .

ELLEN

Don't worry I was just a little bit surprised, that's
   all . . .

*They've gone, laughing softly. Jennifer comes right
into the room. Alceste, of course, now knows she's
there, but remains punishingly silent, nursing his drink.*

JENNIFER

Has something happened? Are you angry?
I get the impression you're mad at me.

ALCESTE

(Give me strength.)

JENNIFER

I'm sorry?

ALCESTE

I said:
Give me strength. So what's he like in bed?

JENNIFER

What?

ALCESTE

Still critical? Or does he lose his objectivity
during exquisite sexual activity?
Was it in this apartment?
I'm beginning to find you physically and morally
   repugnant.

JENNIFER (*strokes his cheek*)

Come on. I bet you say that to all the girls.

ALCESTE

How can you joke about it? The world

170

you inhabit turns betrayal into a game –
only there are no rules, and no sense of shame.
You've just amused yourself with me
(of course, I instinctively
knew that, and everything she's said
confirms things I already
suspected). But I had no real conception
that such effortless deception
was innate.
I warn you: you've chosen the wrong person to
   humiliate.
I accept that you have every right
to love who you like, to spend the night
with who you like. Love – clearly – can't be forced
on someone any more than it can be divorced
from passion. Yes – I understand desire –
but not the chronic need to be a liar.
What was it you said to me?
'Love is a word I don't use lightly'?
If that's the case
then not just love but life itself is meaningless:
and we reach the terminal stage
where there's no feeling left – only rage.
I feel physically sick
just at the thought of it.
You have no soul.
(I think I'd better leave before I lose control.)

JENNIFER

Leave? You can't make serious (I assume) accusations
then just walk out of the situation.

ALCESTE

Really? I should've walked out of this
the moment I became suspicious
instead of falling even more in love
and being made a complete fool of.

JENNIFER

You're intriguing me. I'm completely unaware
of what I've done.

ALCESTE

How can you stand there
and deny the truth
when I have proof?

*He goes to the phone, removes the cassette from the
answering machine and inserts another one from his
pocket. He switches it on. After the beep we hear
Jennifer's voice – in contrast to her usual style, she
sounds hesitant and vulnerable.*

JENNIFER'S VOICE

(*breath*) It's me. Are you there? (*breath*) Look,
I really need to talk. (*breath*) I feel very alone here
and you're my only friend. (*breath*) I just wanted to
hear your voice. Sorry. OK. Call me.

Alceste switches off the machine. Slight pause.

JENNIFER

Where did you get that? You have / no right to –

ALCESTE (*faint laugh*)

Look at you. You've gone completely white.

JENNIFER

Who gave you that? Have you been tapping the phone?

ALCESTE (*mocking*)

'My only friend', 'I feel so alone'.

JENNIFER

Have you?

ALCESTE

You admit it's your voice.

JENNIFER

Yes. Of course. Do I have any *choice*?

ALCESTE

You admit you're having a relationship
with this man – not just a friendship.

JENNIFER

Yes. No. What man? You're going too fast for me.

ALCESTE

Come on, come on: are you asking me
to believe this loving tone
isn't exclusively reserved for our friend Covington?

JENNIFER

Covington? (*faint laugh*) I totally fail to understand.

ALCESTE

My source is impeccable. *And*
it took a great deal of persuasion
believe you me to obtain this information.

JENNIFER

Wait a minute.

Slight pause.

I realise you've somehow gotten this from Marcia . . .
But isn't it obvious the message is for her?

ALCESTE

Oh absolutely. Yes. Obvious.
Please accept my humble apologies.
How dare you insult my intelligence
by twisting the evidence!
Are you really going to try and distort this . . . text
of yours to suggest
you'd be so vulnerable and intimate
with a woman you're widely known to hate?

Well? Shall we listen to it again
while you / attempt to –

> JENNIFER
> I could never explain
anything to you. How dare you assume you have the authority
to invade my privacy?

> ALCESTE
Alright, alright.
Calm down. Let's see you try and shed a favourable
light / on this.

> JENNIFER
You don't own me. It doesn't matter
to me *what* you think. (Don't flatter / yourself.)

> ALCESTE
OK. I'm sorry. Look; just say
what would make you talk to Marcia that way.

> JENNIFER (*coldly and calmly*)
No. It's for Covington.
I've fallen head over heels in love with him.
You're right: he's well-bred
well-read
exquisite (how did you guess?) in bed.
In fact I agree with everything you've said.
Just leave me alone – alright –
then I can get on with fucking every man in sight.

Alceste slaps her face.

You know something: you're completely mad.
I've just lost any respect I ever had
for you. Your assumption of betrayal
is so predictably male
and your resort to violence
speaks volumes. No. Please. Silence

is infinitely preferable to hearing
  how ashamed et cetera et cetera
you now are.
Y'know, what's so endearing
is for me to realise
you've assumed from day one I've been telling lies:
my most intimate confession
of love has been treated throughout with paranoia
  and suspicion.
I tell you I'm in love with you
but, oh no, nothing's ever good enough for you
(and you wonder why I feel isolated and alone
and leave pathetic messages on that woman's phone).
I'm angry.
And I have every right to be.
I naively make a commitment
and in return this is the treatment
I get. (*bitterly*) They say what I do is pornography –
so why don't I stimulate that jealousy
of yours. Yes – why don't I see whether
I can't call some nice young boy right now so you can
  watch us making out together.

ALCESTE

There's nothing remotely naïve
about you. D'you really expect me to believe
this victim acting? Don't you see:
you are my destiny.
I shan't let go:
however low you sink I'm going to follow.

JENNIFER

That's not love, it's a psychiatric *disorder*.

ALCESTE

Maybe, maybe it borders
on it, yes. Sometimes I think the whole idea
of love is mad. The fear

of betrayal, of rejection – the reckless pursuit
of one's own personal humiliation. But the root
goes too deep.
I wish there was a way of keeping
you entirely to myself. Imagine if you were blind,
say, or paralysed. You'd find
out how loyal I was, because then
there'd be no other men
sniffing around. I'm the only one you see who wouldn't
    hurt you
or immediately desert you.
I'd have no rival
and you'd depend on me – literally – for your survival.
Where're you going?

JENNIFER
                You're frightening me.
What kind of weird fantasy
is that?

ALCESTE
    Jennifer.

JENNIFER
        No.
Will you please let go
of me.

He lets go. Pause.

            You've had too much to drink.
OK?

She backs away.

So please: just leave me alone and give me time to think.

She turns suddenly and goes into her bedroom.
Alceste swallows the remainder of his drink.

Act Five

Darkness.

A figure appears carrying a lighted candelabrum. He's dressed as a servant at the court of Louis XIV. He moves round the room and lights more candles.

As the light grows we see that the hotel room has been transformed – by hangings and ornaments – into the baroque. There is an open harpsichord with an erotic painting inside the lid.

As the servant figure – Simon – moves downstage he finds Alceste slumped asleep in a chair. Simon shakes him gently.

SIMON
Monsieur? Monsieur?

Alceste wakes up.

ALCESTE
What the fuck . . .?

SIMON (*mysteriously*)
Voici bien des mystères.

Pause.

ALCESTE
Who are you?

SIMON
Nous sommes mal, Monsieur, dans nos affaires.

ALCESTE
I don't speak French. Why are you dressed like that? I'm sorry but I'm not impressed.

SIMON

Monsieur, il faut faire retraite.

ALCESTE

What?

SIMON

Il faut d'ici déloger sans trompette.

ALCESTE

Speak to me in / English.

SIMON

Il faut partir, Monsieur, sans / dire adieu.

ALCESTE

Speak to me in English will you
or I'll fucking kill you.

*He grabs Simon, but after a moment relaxes his grip.
Simon disdainfully disengages himself and continues
with his preparations of the room.*

I'm sorry. Look I'm sorry I spoke
to you like that.

He looks round the room.

What is this then? Some kind of practical joke?

*John appears, laughing softly. He too is dressed in an
elaborate seventeenth-century costume – and all
subsequent entries will be in costumes in the
extravagant style of Louis' court – the men rivalling the
women. Only Alceste remains in his original clothes.*

JOHN

What's wrong? Have you forgotten about the party?

ALCESTE

Party? I was asleep –
or at least I was until that Gallic creep
woke me up. You're not really dressing up are you?

JOHN

I already have – and I've got something here for you.

He gives Alceste a box.

ALCESTE

What's this?

JOHN

Open it.

ALCESTE

D'you know I was dreaming
of wild animals. They were screaming
and biting into the most vulnerable places
imaginable. Then I saw they all had human faces.

Pause.

What is this?

JOHN

A wig.

ALCESTE (*faint laugh*)
No. I'm sorry.

JOHN

Come on. You're not going to let everybody
down? It would look bad.

ALCESTE

You must be mad
if you think I'm wearing this.

JOHN

It might be an improvement.

ALCESTE

Don't take the piss
out of me.

JOHN
I don't honestly see what harm a / wig can –

ALCESTE
I don't participate in costume fucking drama.

JOHN
Put it on.

ALCESTE
No.

John tries to put the wig on Alceste, who resists with increasing violence.

JOHN
Come on. You're so *uptight*.

ALCESTE
Just take it off. Take it off. I'm not having it. Alright?

He throws the wig down. Pause. John picks it up and smooths it.

JOHN
Was that strictly necessary? Wigs are expensive.
Listen, why / can't you –

ALCESTE
Yes. I know. I'm being childish and offensive
et cetera et cetera. Well let me reimburse you.
Nothing could be worse,
could it, than being in your debt.
Come on. How much? Cash or cheque?

He reaches for his money.

JOHN (*embarrassed*)
Please.

ALCESTE
Everything has a price,

and if my own particular vice
is to express my undying hatred
of human nature, then I'm quite prepared to pay for it.

JOHN

Come *on* . . .

ALCESTE

Come on *what*?
'Be reasonable'? That's about the only argument you've
got.
Can you really tell me to my face
that you love the human race?
Or being in this artificial place?
That you don't dream of somewhere out in space
where this shallow world is not 'all that is the case'?

JOHN

No, no. Absolutely fine.
You don't need (obviously) to read Wittgenstein
to know that even by his or her own evaluation
man is an imperfect creation.
OK?
Our world is shallow. Accepted.
It doesn't follow that you have to reject it.
Surely its very superficiality
is what gives rise to interesting strategies
for survival. If there's no intrinsic meaning
then the fun is to invent one. This evening's
party is a perfect example.
How can you possibly perceive it as harmful?
I'm getting depressed by all your crises.
What good are all your so-called virtues if you can't
enjoy their corresponding vices.

Offers the wig again.

Come on: do it for me.

ALCESTE

I've had enough for one day of your Mr Feel-Good
    philosophy.
Strategies? Meaning? Imperfection?
You have a wonderful gift for self-deception.
You claim academic innocence
while providing the rationale for decadence
of every kind. Every corrupt society enlists
its own tame apologists
and you're turning into one of them:
the kind of person
who paints over a moral mess
with borrowed intellectual fancy-dress.

JOHN

(Please, please, please . . .)

ALCESTE

Look at you. It's embarrassing.

JOHN (*shrugs*)

Embarrassing? It's fun.

ALCESTE

No. I'm sorry. Not everyone
would agree that what went on at Versailles
was 'fun'. Just try
imagining a church and state
monitoring every move you make:
what you write, what you think, who you meet . . .

JOHN

OK, OK. You're still drunk. Why don't you just go
    back to sleep?

ALCESTE

I'm quite sober.
And I tell you: when this party's over
I'm going. And I'm taking Jennifer

out of this. I'm just waiting for
the right moment to tell her. In the morning this will
  just seem

JOHN

I know, I know: like a bad dream.
Fine. Well look, I promised I'd meet Ellen at the desk.

He heads towards the door.

ALCESTE

OK. You know, I'm not depressed
about this. She's going to agree.
I know that secretly she has great respect for me.

JOHN

Absolutely. Well there's no telling
what will happen. I must go down and see Ellen.

John goes out.

*A moment passes. We hear voices and laughter.
Jennifer and Covington emerge from the bedroom, both
in beautiful costumes, Jennifer holding Covington's
script from Act One. They are not aware of Alceste
concealed in the chair downstage.*

COVINGTON

I wrote the part specifically for you.
You know how much I adore
your work.

JENNIFER

  Well, thank you.

COVINGTON

    And perhaps if you could use your
influence and show this to a producer . . .?
It's conceived for the stage but could be
very easily developed into a full-scale movie.

Pause. He looks at her.

JENNIFER

What is it?

COVINGTON (*lowers voice*)
　　　　Alceste. Can I be very personal
and ask if the two of you . . .? It's just there are some awful
rumours going round and I wondered if there was any truth in it.
(By the way: he's not to know you've got this script.)

JENNIFER (*faint laugh*)
Are you hitting on me?
I don't understand. And why the need for secrecy?

COVINGTON

Certain things are best
left unexplained. But it's no secret that I detest
him. (*He takes her hand.*) And the fact is
– yes – I find you extremely extremely attractive.

ALCESTE (*reveals himself*)
I'm *sure* you do. And it's obviously mutual
judging from the way you're blushing like a schoolgirl.
You talk about commitment and you let him
into your *bed*room
to what? Discuss his play?
Come on. I wasn't born yesterday.

COVINGTON

Can we please deal with this rationally.
I have no intention of trespassing on your territory.

ALCESTE

And I have no intention of waiting
here watching you salivating.

COVINGTON

She obviously prefers Neanderthals.

ALCESTE

No no. She clearly prefers the company of fools.

COVINGTON (*goes to Jennifer*)

I won't make a scene. He's obviously frightened.

ALCESTE

You? Make a scene? You can't even *write* one.

COVINGTON (*to Jennifer*)

I really think you ought to intervene.

ALCESTE (*to Jennifer*)

I think it's time you told us what / all this *means*.

COVINGTON

Isn't there some way of / *pacifying* him?

ALCESTE

Refusing to speak isn't going to satisfy anyone.

COVINGTON

You're not really in love with this paralytic?

ALCESTE

You're not really sleeping – are you – with a critic?

JENNIFER

Boys, boys. It must be time for your medication.
I feel like I'm in an institution watching the patients.
D'you really think I'm such a child
that I can't make up my own mind?
D'you both respect me so little
that resolving your own quarrel
is more important than considering my feelings?
Quite frankly nothing could be less appealing
to me than your undisguised

jealousy. And someone's going to be unpleasantly
    surprised
when they *do* see
the real me.
If you were even remotely sensitive –
either of you – you'd know that I'm being tentative
only because I find you both rather scary.

To Alceste.

And what's wrong with you? You haven't said a word
    about what I'm wearing.

COVINGTON

Then let me apologise. But even so
you can't equivocate.

ALCESTE

                    And I have a *right* to know.
Just what *is* the truth?
What *is* the 'real you'?
The dress,
yes,
is very beautiful . . .

JENNIFER

Thank you.

ALCESTE

. . . but entirely – and stunningly – superficial.
If this . . . man really is your lover
then obviously our relationship is over.
I apologise for my previous (yes, I'm sorry) violence
but please see that you no longer have a right to silence.

COVINGTON

Absolutely. Prevaricating
like this is simply self-incriminating.

JENNIFER

Oh, is that a fact?

186

What is this? Some kind of British neo-fascist double-
act?
I've told you: you'll both just have to keep waiting.
Ellen! My *God*! You look totally *devastating*!

Ellen has appeared in costume, accompanied by John.
Laughing, she kisses cheeks with Jennifer.

I'm so pleased to see you. I had visions
of being burned by the Inquisition
here. These two charming creatures
are worse than the Society of fucking Jesus.
Thank God I have an ally.
Look at them: can't you see they're just dying
to get the thumbscrews out.

ELLEN (*tries to take her aside*)
Listen, there's something we need to talk about.

JENNIFER (*laughing*)
Seriously. I was scared.

ELLEN (*as before*)
No. Listen. I think you need to be prepared / for this.

COVINGTON
Is there something we're not supposed to hear?

JENNIFER
Can't you just fuck off for a moment. Go on. /
Disappear.

ALCESTE
Don't talk to him like that. You've no right / to be
abusive.

JENNIFER
No right? Since when did you acquire this interest in
what is or is not polite?
Give me some space, OK? I just want

187

to speak privately to my . . . whatever you are.

ELLEN

Confidante.

JENNIFER

Confidante. Exactly.

Before they can speak, Julian, Alex and Marcia – all costumed – enter brusquely, carrying bundles of the evening paper, which they dump on the floor.

JULIAN

Well, well, well. They do indeed exist:
the mythical female icon and the uncompromising
   journalist.

ALEX (*coldly*)

Jenny darling, what a wonderful dress.
And Ellen – let's all drink shall we to the freedom of
   the gutter press.

Alex and Simon hand out champagne over the following.

ELLEN

(I tried to / warn you.)

MARCIA

Yes, yes, yes. I know you can't stand the sight of me
but remember darling, you did invite me.
I was just gluing on my beauty spot
when I got
the most amazing phone call from Alex
asking me if I'd seen the evening paper.
               Of course we all know how he panics –
don't you Alex – so of course I read the piece
expecting it to be just sleaze,
the usual nasty prying journalese.
But unless you've been seriously misquoted

then even someone like myself . . . a devoted
friend . . . I mean I'm all for speaking one's mind,
but . . .

JULIAN

I think you're being far too kind,
Marcia. The whole thing quite frankly stinks.

ALEX

I mean if this is really what she thinks / of us . . .

JULIAN

I don't know which is more demeaning:
saying it or printing it. Yes, we've all been
hurt sometimes by the papers – but never attacked
like this. Let me read a typical extract:
'It's awesome to be sitting just feet away from a young
    woman whose controversial screen performances
    have divided the critics and become iconic for
    generation X . . .'
blah blah blah . . .
'My first question is about her relationship with
    superbrat –'
thank you very much
'– actor Julian St John Smith, a frequent visitor to
    her luxury penthouse suite. She is surprisingly frank.'
and I quote:
' "Julian is a kind of caricature of all the bad things
you hear about the English – inbred, class-obsessed,
vain and emotionally retarded. He's also a terrible
actor." '
Unquote.

JENNIFER

Ellen, this was *not part* of the interview.

JULIAN

Excuse me. May I continue?

'I ask her what it's like to meet Covington, a critic who
    has consistently championed her work on this side of
    the Atlantic. She gives a sphinx-like smile and says:'
quote
'Menopausal male critics have a tendency to admire
    any young woman who takes her clothes off in front
    of the camera. I'm sure he was thrilled to meet me
    but I can't say that the thrill was mutual.'
Unquote.

JENNIFER

I don't understand. You've abused our friendship.

MARCIA

You should be more careful who you get into bed with.

ALEX (*takes over reading*)

'Over vodka martinis on the roof garden with its
    stunning panorama of the river the conversation
    turns to top actors' agent Alexander Alvi. Is it true,
    I ask, that without Alex she'd never have made the
    transition to major star status? Her response is
    refreshingly blunt: "Alex's input into my career has
    been less than zero. He has his own reasons for
    cultivating me – well two reasons to be precise –
    greed and lust." I ask I her finally . . .'

JENNIFER

Alex . . .

Slight pause.

ALEX

'I ask her finally to comment on her much-rumoured
    relationship with writer Alceste. Is he, I suggest,
    a kind of father-figure to her? She stares for a while
    into her glass before gazing up at me with her cool
    blue eyes. "I can't think of anyone," she says, "less
    like my father, who is gentle, quiet, respected and

respectful of others. Alceste thinks of himself as
a kind of misanthrope, but I suspect that at heart
he's just another good old-fashioned misogynist."
Her outspoken self-confidence makes it hard to
believe that this beautiful young woman has only
just emerged from her teens . . .'
Et cetera et cetera.

He lets the paper fall. Silence.

JENNIFER

I thought we were friends, Ellen. I invited you here as
a *guest*.

ELLEN

I have my career to think of – and I do believe this is
in the public interest.

ALEX

Well Jenny, you are a real model of loyalty –
what wonderful news for the whole agency.
(We're going to need more than lawyers to handle
this kind of scandal.)

JULIAN

Great article. *Loved* the style.
No, I really don't think it's worth my while
getting angry. Who cares about you and your dykey
friend when I can have any woman I bloody well like.

COVINGTON

And what about my script?
She promised me she'd commit to it!
She's obviously made so many promises
they've become meaningless.
Well, I've behaved like a complete idiot
haven't I? But at least you've made me realise it
in time. I'm sure you'll always be in the news,
Jenny. Just don't expect any more good reviews.

To Alceste.

I apologise for what happened earlier on today.
Obviously I have no intention of standing in your way.

MARCIA

I came here as you can imagine fully intending
to take your side – desperately wanting to defend
you – but you are clearly, my darling, morally deformed.
And I have to say to everyone: you *were* warned.
(And how anyone could write this kind of feature
with no reference whatsoever to Jenny's most
    significant teacher . . .)
But the person who must be the most cut up
and hurt is this poor man / whose integrity –

ALCESTE

                                        Just shut up
will you for once. You're not my wife,
and you can kindly keep your nose out of my
    emotional life.
Don't think I don't know the price
you're asking for taking my side in this –
a considerable amount
(and I don't think I could bring myself to settle the
    account).

MARCIA

Don't flatter yourself. *Wife?* What makes you think
    I'd want to be
sold into paternalistic slavery
with you? Marriage is just an anachronism
darling – a relic of late-twentieth-century capitalism
or didn't you know? And I think I'd be afraid to get
    my kicks
from Jennifer's rejects.
(After all I'm not someone who happily caters
for people of dubious immunological status.)

I have no wish to 'come between you' whatsoever
and I'm sure you'll be terribly terribly terribly happy
  together.

ALCESTE

So. You've all had your little say
then, just like in an old play
where everyone makes a speech.

Pause.

                            And now it's my turn,
only for once / I . . .

JENNIFER
                    OK, OK everyone, burn
me then, at the stake. You're after
blood – clearly – and hey! I'm the martyr.
Mistakes have been made – yes –
and I can see that this is where I'm expected to confess
et cetera et cetera and beg forgiveness.
But as God is my witness
I'm no more guilty of deception
than any other person standing in this room –
with perhaps one notable exception.

To Alceste.

You're the only one here who doesn't take me
for granted. And you have every right to hate me.
I'm sorry.

ALCESTE
                    D'you think I'm so disloyal
as to judge you by a sound-bite in a newspaper article?
It's obvious to me you've been provoked
into making these comments. (*to Ellen*) And I'd've
  hoped
that for all your intellectual wheeler-dealing

193

you might have spared some thought for this girl's
   feelings.
How you can vandalise
a person's soul in search of scandal is
beyond me. Fortunately the truth of human
nature can't be condensed into your squalid little
   column.

To Jennifer.

Listen: we have so much in common:
we're quick to be judgemental
and both unfashionably sentimental
and this is what I propose:
no more films, acting, parties, interviews.
Quit the city. Forget work. Turn our backs
on all of this. Begin to relax.
Just the two of us.
We can become anonymous.
We'll buy a little house
with a garden – trees – a stream – whatever.
Then we could think about starting – don't you see –
   a / family together.

JENNIFER (*crescendo of disbelief*)
No, no, no, no, no, no, no . . . *What? Leave?*
What're you trying to *do* to me? This is the air I breathe.

ALCESTE
We don't *need* these people. This hotel,
these costumes – it's like an ante-room to hell.
Look at them, Jennifer. *They* don't care.

JENNIFER (*faint laugh*)
You're seriously asking me to join you in some kind of
   suburban nightmare?
Shop? Cook? Clean? What? Do the dishes? *Sleep?*
Drive the kids to ballet in a Japanese *jeep?*

Ellen laughs softly.

'These people' are still (I hope) my friends – *and* –
like it or not – this is the world I understand.

*She takes Ellen's arm. The others grin, now they see
the tide is turning against Alceste.*

Maybe right now they're temporarily
a little mad at me –
but I know they'll soon enough forgive me.
Won't you?

ALEX (*smiling*)

Jenny . . .

She offers her hand to Alex. He laughs and kisses it.

JENNIFER

Don't you see?
And Julian – he *loves* to be my slave
really – kicked, whipped and made to behave –
don't you boy? It's a sado-masochistic need
entirely characteristic of the breed.

*Julian lets his tongue hang out and pants rapidly like
a dog. Jennifer laughs and offers her hand. He kisses
it languorously. She strokes his face. Everyone except
Alceste laughs. Without releasing Julian she turns to
Alceste.*

It might've been fun for us to have an *affair,*
but I've just turned twenty, and I'm not *going* anywhere.

The others all laugh softly.

(*intensely*) I love the city – and the night.
And no way will I abandon them without a fight.
Simon.

SIMON

Madame?

JENNIFER

He makes such a wonderful
servant and his French is impeccable.
Let's have some music. And nothing too arty.
I'm sick of this. I want to party.

*The others laugh. Simon begins to play boogie-woogie
on the harpsichord, but after a moment Alceste makes
a violent gesture – bangs down the lid, or smashes a
plaster Cupid – and the music stops.*

ALCESTE

If that's the life you want to lead,
so be it. Just don't come to me when you need
help, because I shan't be there.
You may not believe in despair
but I do. It's a kind of pit
and you're digging yourself deeper and deeper into it.

He walks out. Embarrassed laughter.

JOHN

It's so typical of him to overreact.
Don't worry: I'll run and bring him straight back.

*John moves towards the exit but, at an imperceptible
gesture from Jennifer, Simon and Alex block his way.*

What're you doing? Look: I want to leave.
I'm worried about him.

ELLEN

Relax, John, just relax. Don't you see
we're better off without him.

ATTEMPTS ON HER LIFE

'No one will have directly experienced
the actual cause of such happenings,
but everyone will have received
an image of them.'

Baudrillard

Seventeen Scenarios for the Theatre

Attempts on her Life was first presented at the Royal Court Theatre Upstairs, London, on 7 March 1997, with the following cast:

Kacey Ainsworth
Danny Cerqueira
David Fielder
Ashley Jensen
Hakeem Kae-Kazim
Etela Pardo
Sandra Voe
Howard Ward

Directed by Tim Albery
Designed by Gideon Davey
Lighting by Simon Mills
Music composed by David Benke
Sound by Paul Arditti
Choreography by Patti Powell

This is a piece for a company of actors
whose composition should reflect the composition
of the world beyond the theatre.

A dash (—) at the beginning of a line indicates
a change of speaker. If there is no dash after a pause,
it means the same character is still speaking.

A slash (/) marks the point of interruption in
overlapping dialogue.

In performance, the first scenario,
ALL MESSAGES DELETED, may be cut.

I ALL MESSAGES DELETED

beep

— Anne. (*pause*) It's me. (*pause*) I'm calling from
Vienna. (*pause*) No, sorry; I'm calling from . . .
Prague. (*pause*) It's Prague. (*pause*) I'm pretty sure it's
Prague. Anyway, look . . . (*breath*) Anne . . . (*breath*)
I want to apologise. (*breath*) I realise how much I've
hurt you, my sweet sweet darling, and . . . (*breath*)
Ah. Look. Look, there's somebody on the other line,
Anne. I really really – I'm sorry – but I really really
have to take this call. I'll get back to you.

'*Monday 8.53 a.m.*'

beep

— Anne. Hi. Listen. I only have a moment. Are you
there? No? Okay. Look. It's this. What we were
discussing? You remember? Well what about this,
what about this, what about if, let's say, let's say, let's
just say . . . that the trees have names? Okay? That's
right – the trees. You think – I know – you think I'm
crazy. But let's just accept for a moment shall we that
the trees have names. Then what if, what if, what
about if . . . *this was her tree.* Shit. Sorry. Look, I
have to board now. But think about that. The trees
have names. And one of them is hers. I have to run.

'*Monday 9.35 a.m.*'

beep

— (*spoken in e.g. Czech*) You know who this is. You
leave the device in a small truck at the back of the
building. You'll get the truck from Barry. Barry will
contact you with more instructions.

'*Monday 11.51 a.m.*'

beep

— . . . Oh. Hello? It's Mum . . .

'*Monday 1.05 p.m.*'

beep

— Hello, this is Sally at Cooper's. Just to let you know
that the vehicle is now in the showroom and ready
for your collection. Thank you.

'*Monday 1.06 p.m.*'

beep

— We know where you live you fucking bitch. You're
dead, basically. The things you fucking did. We don't
forget. (*pause*) You'll wish you'd never been *born*.

'*Monday 1.32 p.m.*'

beep

— . . . Anne? Hello? It's Mum again. (*pause*) Got your
postcard. (*pause*) Looks very nice. (*pause*) And the
photo. Is that really you? (*pause*) Glad you're making
friends and so on. (*pause*) The thing is, Anne, there
just isn't any money to send you. I've spoken to your
dad, and he says no, absolutely not.

*We hear a man's voice in the background: 'Not
another penny. Just you make that clear.' Mum*

*replies: 'I'm telling her, I'm telling her.' Then back
into the phone:*

I'm really sorry, Anne darling, but we just can't keep
on doing it.

*Man's voice again: 'If you don't tell her, I'll bloody
well talk to her.'*

Look, I have to go now, darling. Your dad sends his
love. All right? God bless.

'Monday 2.20 p.m.'

beep

— Anne? Are you there? Pick up the phone, Annie.
(*pause*) Okay . . . It's a quarter after ten here in
Minnesota and we're just calling to say our thoughts
and prayers are with you, Annie. And we love you
very much.

'Monday 4.13 p.m.'

beep

— Anne? Brilliant. It's moving. It's timely. It's distressing.
It's funny. It's sexy. It's deeply serious. It's entertaining.
It's illuminating. It's cryptic. It's dark. Let's meet.
Call me.

'Monday 10.21 p.m.'

beep

— Anne. Good evening. Let me tell you what I'm going
to do to you. First you're going to suck my cock. Then
I'm going to fuck you up the arse. With a broken
bottle. And that's just for starters. Little miss cunt.

'Monday 10.30 p.m.'

beep

— Anne?

Pick up the phone. (*pause*) I know you're there. (*pause*) It's no use hiding, Anne. Hiding from what? (*pause*) The world? Hiding from the world, Anne? Come *on*. Grow up. Grow up, Anne, and pick up the phone.

Pause.

So what is this then? A cry for help? Don't tell me this is a cry for help. Because what am *I* supposed to do exactly about *your* cry for help? Mm? (*pause*) And what if you're lying there, Anne, already dead? Mm?

Is that the scenario I'm supposed to imagine?

The scenario of a dead body rotting next to the machine?

Faint laugh Pause.

The what, the larvae of flies listening to your messages? Or if your building has been destroyed. Or if your city has been destroyed.
The airports and the shoe shops. The theatres and the fashionable halogen-lit cafés that have sprung up in the disused warehouses by the disused canals. Mm?

Faint laugh.

So only the larvae of insects are listening to your messages. Listening to me, Anne, as they tunnel through your remains.

Pause.

I'm growing morbid, Anne.
I think you should pick up the phone and make me smile, make me smile the way you used to, Anne.

I know you're there.
I know you're there, Anne. And I know that if I'm
patient, you'll answer me.

Pause.

You will answer me, won't you Anne.

'Tuesday 12.19 a.m.'

*'That was your last message.
To save all messages press one.'*

Pause.

'All messages deleted.'

2 TRAGEDY OF LOVE AND IDEOLOGY

— Summer. A river. Europe. These are the basic ingredients.

— And a river running through it.

— A river, exactly, running through a great European city and a couple at the water's edge. These are the basic ingredients.

— The woman?

— Young and beautiful, naturally.

— The man?

— Older, troubled, sensitive, naturally.

— A naturally sensitive man but nevertheless a man of power and authority who knows that this is wrong.

— They both know this is wrong.

— They both know this is wrong but they can't / help themselves. Exactly.

— They're making love in the man's apartment.

— Doing what?

— Making love. Making love in the man's apartment. A luxury apartment, naturally, with a view over the entire city. These are the / basic ingredients.

— A panorama of the entire city. The charming geometry of the rooftops. The skylights and the quaint chimneys. And beyond the TV aerials are monuments of culture: the Duomo of Florence and

the arch at La Défense, Nelson's Column and the
Brandenburg Gate / to name but four.

— The woman cries out. Her golden hair cascades as it
were over the edge of the bed. She grips the
bed-frame. Her knuckles whiten. There are tears / in
her eyes.

— The apartment is beautifully furnished.

— Well obviously the apartment would be beautifully
furnished. Obviously it would have high ceilings and
tall windows and date in all probability date from
the end of the nineteenth century when the rise in
speculative building coincided with the aspirations
of the liberal bourgeoisie to create monumental
architectural schemes such as I'm thinking particularly
now I'm thinking of the Viennese Ringstrasse which
made such an impression on the young Adolf Hitler
as he stood one morning / before the Opera.

— Or one of the great Parisian / boulevards.

— Or one of the great, exactly, Parisian / boulevards.

— And meanwhile, as you say, her golden hair cascades
as it were over the edge of the bed. She grips the
frame. Her knuckles whiten and her pupils widen,
while he –

— Let's say he grunts.

— Grunts?

— Let's say he grunts, yes, but sensitively. Let's say it's
the sensitive grunt of the attractive man of power and
authority, not for example the coarse pig-like grunt of
a mechanic lying on his back in a confined space
trying to loosen a cross-threaded nut with a heavy
and inappropriately sized wrench.

— Absolutely not.

— Absolutely not, but the masterful grunt of a man who breakfasts on one continent and lunches on another, who flies first class with a linen napkin and a comprehensive wine list.

— That kind of man.

— That kind of grunt.

— That kind of light.

— What kind of light?

— The kind of light that streams in. It streams in through the tall windows transforming their bodies into a kind of golden mass.

— A writhing mass.

— The light, the golden mass, these are the / essential ingredients.

— But now a look crosses her face.

— A what?

— A look.

— A doubt.

— A look of doubt, yes, good, crosses Anne's face.

— Even now.

— Even now in the / intensity of her passion.

— Even now in the intensity of her passion a kind of shadow crosses her face.

— A premonitory shadow.

— Premonitory?

— A premonitory shadow, yes, crosses her face.

— Is that a word?

— Is what a word?

Pause.

— Well yes, of course premonitory / is a word.

— Later. Night.

— The lights of the city at night. Strings of light, suspended star-like along the quays and the frameworks of bridges. Odd dull red warning lights pulsing on the tops of tower blocks and TV transmitters. The man at the telephone. His lowered voice. His troubled glances.

— Anne wakes up in the solid walnut bed, hears his faint male voice in the adjoining room. The exquisite Louis Quatorze clock beside her chimes three by means of a tiny tiny naked gilt shepherd striking a tiny tiny golden bell held between the teeth of an enamelled wolf, no doubt a reference to an ancient myth well known to the seventeenth-century French nobility but now totally erased from human consciousness.

— Ting ting ting.

Pause.

— 3 a.m. Anne wakes up. Hears voice, lights cigarette. Appears in doorway. Dialogue.

— Who was it, she says.

— Nothing, he says.

— Who the fuck was it, she says. End of dialogue.

— And now she's angry – exactly: end of dialogue – and now she's angry. She's angry because she knows exactly who it is.

— His political masters / calling him.

— His political masters, that's right, calling him. Just as they have always called him. The very political masters that she hates with every fibre as it were of her being. The very men and women, that she, Anne, in her youthful idealism holds responsible for the terminal injustice of this world.

— The leaders who in her naïve and passionate opinion have destroyed everything she values in the name (a) of business and (b) of laissez-faire.

— In the name (a) of rationalization and (b) / of enterprise.

— In the name of (a) so-called individualism and (b) / of so-called choice.

— The basic ingredients in other words of a whole tragedy.

— A whole, exactly, tragedy unfolds before our eyes in Paris, Prague, Venice or Berlin to name but four, as the moon, vast and orange, rises over the renaissance domes, baroque palaces, nineteenth-century zoos and railway stations, and modernist slabs of social housing exemplifying the dictum *form follows function*.

— Form follows function.

— This whole tragedy / of love.

— This whole tragedy of ideology and love.

— She stubs out the cigarette.

— She begins to shout.

— She begins to beat him with her fists.

— She begins to bite him with her teeth.

— She begins to kick him with her bare white feet.

— She beats and beats / and beats.

— She beats and beats. And the exquisite clock which has survived two revolutions and three centuries is smashed to pieces on the smooth and highly polished parquet as she beats bites and kicks.

— The tiny tiny shepherd and the tiny tiny bell both vanish – rather a nice touch this – vanish for ever under the / walnut bed.

— Until she stops for breath. Let's say she finally, shall we, stops, at this point, for breath.

— The woman?

— The woman, Anne, yes, stops for breath.

Pause.

— And he?

— Bows his head.

— Yes.

— Looks up at her.

— Yes.

— Takes her tear-stained / face between his hands.

— Takes Anne's tear-stained face between his hands like a precious chalice.

— Or a rugby football.

— Like a precious silver chalice or as you say a rugby football before a drop-kick he takes Anne's angry tear-stained face between his hands.

— He still loves her.

— For all their ideological differences – that's right – he still loves her. Speech.

— One day, Anne, he says, you'll understand my world. One day, Anne, you'll understand that everything must be paid for, that even your ideals must finally be paid for. End of speech. At which he smoothes the wet strands of hair from her lips and kisses her. These are the / basic ingredients.

— He kisses her and presses her back down onto the bed. Or she him. Better still: *she* presses *him* back down onto the bed such is her emotional confusion, such is her sexual appetite, such is her inability to distinguish between right and wrong in this great consuming passion in the high-ceilinged apartment with the solid walnut bed, the polished parquet floor, the grand piano by Pleyel circa 1923 without it should perhaps be noted any visible means of protection against pregnancy in the case of Anne or in the case of either against sexually transmitted diseases including the so-called AIDS virus more correctly known as the human immune deficiency virus or / HIV for short.

— A portrait of a young girl sketching once thought to be by David but now attributed to his female contemporary Constance Charpentier, and a triangular yellow ashtray with the legend 'Ricard' containing three cigarette butts and a quantity of fine grey ash.

Pause.

— A great tragedy in other words / of love.

— A great – exactly – tragedy of ideology / and love.

— These are the basic ingredients.

3 FAITH IN OURSELVES

Silence.

— The whole of the past is there in her face. It's written
there like a history. The history of her family. The
history of the land itself – this land where her family
has lived for generations.

Silence.

— It's a valley.

— It's a valley – yes – deep in the hills.

— It's a valley deep in the hills where the traditional
ways have been maintained for generations. And there
are fruit trees.

— Each child who is born in this valley has a fruit tree
planted in their name. In fact there's a kind of
ceremony.

— A formal – exactly – ceremony.

— A kind of formal ceremony takes place in the village.
And for generation upon generation this formal
ceremony of naming has taken place on the birth
of each child.

— The trees in other words have names.

— They have names just as the inhabitants have names.
There is the person, and there is the tree. There is
Anya the woman, and there is Anya the tree.

— The trees have names and so do the blades, the blades
of grass. Because life is so precious, life is so *felt,*

things are so *alive*, so *sacred*, that even the blades of grass have names. It's something we can hardly *comprehend*.

— We can hardly comprehend this sacred sacred life, this sense of completeness is beyond our understanding, this sense of awe humbles us.

— But now, devastation.

Silence.

— What?

— Devastation. The harmony of generations / has been destroyed.

— Exactly. This enclosed, secure world has been torn apart.

— The harmony of generations has been destroyed. The women have been raped. The little children have been disembowelled.

— The women have been raped, and then disembowelled. The men have hacked each other to pieces.

— Brother has killed brother.

— Cousin has murdered cousin. Brother has raped sister.

— Brother has raped – yes – sister, and now the dogs are picking over the remains.

— The petrol used to fuel the ancient tractors and generate electricity for the old black-and-white TVs has been used to set people alight.

— Yes.

— First to set living people alight, and now, for health reasons, to burn the corpses.

— Living people set on fire. The cold vapour of the petrol, then the hot rush of flame. The burning people running blazing between the fruit trees which bear their names, scorching the leaves, writhing on the blades of grass, while the soldiers stand by laughing.

— The soldiers are laughing even though these are their own cousins, their own *parents*, their / mothers and fathers.

— Burning their own *parents* in the sacred orchard. Burning them alive and laughing.

— Or burying them alive. Burying them alive up to their necks in the fertile earth, then smashing their skulls open with a spade. They have a name for this.

— 'The flower.'

— It's called, that's right, 'the flower'.

Silence.

And it's all there in her face.

— It's what?

— All there. All there in her face.

— In Anya's face. We don't need words. She's beyond words. Her mouth, in fact her mouth trembles but no words come.

— The inadequacy of words.

— The terrifying, yes, inadequacy of words as she stands by a tree covered in delicate white petals.

— A plum.

— A plum tree covered in delicate white petals which is the moment . . .

— Yes.

— . . . the moment we realise that *this is her tree.*

— This is *her own tree,* Anya's tree.

— Anya's tree, planted what? forty? fifty? years ago on the day of her birth. The hole dug by her father, the roots spread out by her mother and watered and tended by the family who now lie dead.

— Her very own tree.

— The air still smells of petrol.

— It's spring.

Silence.

— Panorama of the whole valley.

— The whole deep valley in spring.

— The trees. The grass.

— A bee crawls into the cup of a flower.

— And now she speaks.

— Yes. Because she *must.* Because the words well up as she stands beside her tree.

— The tree gives her strength, the strength / to speak.

— She points to some charred timbers. That, she says, was my home. My children were hiding under the bed. They killed them both. First the boy. Then the girl. They set light to my little girl's hair. I still don't know why they set light to my little girl's hair. It crackled like a pile of sticks.

— Then she breaks down.

— Who? Anya?

— She screams. She breaks down and scratches her cheeks like something / from an ancient tragedy.

— I don't think so. I don't think Anya screams. I don't think she breaks down and scratches her cheeks like something from an ancient tragedy. I think her eyes blaze. I think she advances towards the camera and begins to curse. You mother-fucking shit-faced murderers, she says. You pig-fucking cock-sucking bastards. You sister-fucking blaspheming child-murdering mindless fuck-faced killers. I spit on your graves and on the graves of your mothers and fathers and curse all future generations.

— She's angry.

— She's very angry.

Silence.

She's very angry, but she has a *right* to be.

— She has – well obviously – a right to be angry. Everything destroyed. A way of *life* destroyed. A relationship / with *nature* destroyed.

— And this is why we sympathise.

— Of *course* we sympathise.

— Not just sympathise, but *empathise.* Empathise because . . .

— Yes.

— . . . because Anya's valley is *our* valley. Anya's trees are *our* trees. Anya's family is the family to which we all belong.

— So it's a universal thing / *obviously.*

— It's a universal thing in which we recognise, we strangely recognise ourselves. Our own world. Our own pain.

— Our own anger.

— A universal thing which strangely . . . what? what? what?

— Which strangely restores.

— Which strangely restores – I think it does – yes – our faith in ourselves.

4 THE OCCUPIER

— She's the kind of person who believes the message on the till receipt.

— 'Thank you for your custom.'

— She never stands forward of this notice . . .

— Never.

— . . . or speaks to the driver.

Pause.

— When a letter comes addressed to 'The Occupier', she first of all makes . . .

— What? A cup of tea?

— Yes. Then sits at the kitchen table to open it. She opens it and reads it as carefully as if it were a letter from her own son, who now lives in America.

— Canada, actually.

— She's the kind of person who believes the lucky numbers have / been selected . . .

— Toronto.

— . . . just for her. Which in a way, of course, they have. And if she replies within ten days, she will receive a mystery gift. / Toronto? Is it?

— It's not a mystery gift, no. She ticks a *box,* she ticks a *box selecting* the gift she wants to receive: maybe a handy clock-radio, a camera or a set of / miniature screwdrivers.

— A set of miniature screwdrivers or a handy disposable camera.

— She's a non-smoker.

Silence.

— She's definitely a non-smoker. Although I think it's true to say she may occasionally take cigarettes from other people.

— Exactly. At parties.

5 THE CAMERA LOVES YOU

The camera *loves* you
The camera *loves* you
The camera *loves* you

We *need* to sympathise
We *need* to empathise
We *need* to advertise
We *need* to realise
We are the good guys
We are the good guys

We need to feel
what we're seeing is real
It isn't just acting
it's far more exacting
than acting
We're talking reality
We're talking humanity
We're talking of a plan to be
OVERWHELMED by the sheer totality
and utterly believable three-dimensionality
THREE-DIMENSIONALITY
of all the things that Anne can be
ALL THE THINGS THAT ANNE CAN BE

What's Hecuba to him or he to Hecuba?
A megastar
A MEGASTAR

The camera *loves* you
The camera *loves* you
The camera *loves* you

223

We *need* to fantasise
We *need* to improvise
We *need* to synthesise

We *need* to advertise that
We are the good guys
We are the good guys

We need to go
for the sexiest scenario
It isn't just writing
it's much more exciting
than writing
We're talking actuality
We're talking contemporary
We're saying that we want to be
OVERWHELMED by the sheer quantity
YES BY THE SHEER QUANTITY
of all the things that Anne can be
ALL THE THINGS THAT ANNE CAN BE

What's Hecuba to her or she to Hecuba?
A megastar
(A megastar? The fuck you are)

The camera loves you
The camera loves you
The camera the camera
the camera the camera
the camera the camera
THE CAMERA LOVES YOU

6 MUM AND DAD

— It's not her first attempt.

— It shouldn't be her first attempt. She's tried at various times. Even before she leaves home / she tries, doesn't she?

— She tries at various times throughout her *life*.

— We see the other times.

— We live *through* the other times. We live through these harrowing times.

Silence.

— We see photos, don't we.

— We see large numbers of photos.

— We see them close to, so close you can make out the little dots. Funny, isn't it, how everything at a certain point turns into just these little dots – even her smile.

— It's a happy smile. It's a genuine enough smile.

— Oh yes, it's a genuinely happy / smile alright.

— Because no one's *forcing* her, no one's forcing her to smile, are they?

— No one's forcing her to do *anything*. The idea of Annie, little Annie being forced to do things is quite frankly ludicrous.

— No question of it.

Silence. In the silence:

        'She enjoys hosting these holidays
        because she loves meeting people.
    She will introduce you to your fellow guests
    ensuring that everyone has a memorable time.'

— Absolutely – and this should be made clear – absolutely no question of her doing what she does not / want to do.

— Everything at a certain point turns into these little dots – eyes, hair, smile.

— Smiles from all over the world.

— *People* from all over the world. People from all over the world photographed with Annie. Smiling with Annie. Characters I suppose who just popped in and / out of her life.

— And then popped out again.

— And then – yes – popped straight out again.

— Porno, actually, some of them.

— Porno? Come on. Hardly.

— Pretty pornographic, actually, some / of those pictures.

— I'd hardly call it pornographic, just high spirits. Just the high spirits you'd expect of a girl who's always smiling, always laughing, always on the move, always meeting someone, always leaving someone, always in a departure lounge or a bus station or waiting by an airport carousel or sleeping in the corridor / of a train.

— Always by the side of the road somewhere with that big red bag of hers. Somewhere in Africa, say, with that big red canvas bag she got from Mum and Dad

when she turned sixteen. Somewhere in South
America.

— Somewhere in Europe with that big / red bag.

— Europe. Africa, South America, you name it. Brazil.

— Cuba. Brazil. Romania. / *Nigeria.*

— Romania. Cuba. Florida. Australia.

— That's right. Australia. New Zealand. The / Philippines.

— Morocco. Algeria. Tunisia. The Sahara Desert.

— The Kalahari Desert, the foothills of the Himalayas.

— The foothills of the Alps.

— That's right – the what's it called –

— The / Piedmont.

— The Piedmont. Always in some foothills somewhere
with that big red bag of hers.

— Because, let's face it, she *is* concerned.

— Well of *course* she's concerned. We can *see* that she's
concerned. You only have to see her for example in
those photos, the way she's rubbing shoulders with
the poor. She's not afraid in those photos to rub
shoulders with the poor.

— Pictures of her in slums with the smiling slum-dwellers.

— Pictures of her on hillsides with the smiling hill-
dwellers.

— Pictures of her – exactly – with the smiling hill-
dwellers whose land has been eroded, just swept off –
fwah! – by the wind.

— And on rubbish dumps.

— Pictures of Annie on rubbish dumps next to smiling people actually living on the dumps, actually living right there on the dumps / with their *children*.

— Whole families of gypsies or whatever they are, are apparently living, that's right, right there on the dumps.

— What it's not – and this is perhaps how it differs from those previous attempts – what it's not is a cry for help.

— It's quite clear that her mind's / made up.

— It's not a cry for help. It's very important to establish that, wouldn't you agree, from the outset. It's very important to establish that no one could've helped / her at that point.

— No one could've helped her – not her Mum – not her Dad – and certainly none of her so-called / *friends*.

— She wouldn't've / *wanted* help.

— Help is the last thing she would've wanted.

Silence. In the silence:

> 'She enjoys spending lots of time with guests,
> and gets a feeling of great satisfaction
> when everyone is having a good time.
> She says there are lots of hugs at the station
> when it's time to go home, with holidaymakers
> waving and calling out
> "see you next time" from the train window.'

They laugh all through next passage:

— Some of the strange things she says . . .

— Some of the strange things she says to her Mum and Dad as a child: 'I feel like a screen.'

— 'I feel like a screen.'

— She's lying there, isn't she, with the tube in her poor thin arm, looking terribly pale, whiter in fact than / the *pillow*.

— 'Like a TV screen,' she says, 'where everything from the front looks real and alive, but round the back there's just dust and a few wires.'

— 'Dust and a few wires.' Her imagination . . .

— She says she's not a real character, not a real character like you get in a book or on TV, but a *lack* of character, an *absence* she calls it, doesn't she, of character.

— An absence of character, whatever *that* means . . .

— *Then* she wants to be a terrorist, doesn't she?

— That's right. She comes down one night to the kitchen with those big earnest eyes of hers and tells her Mum and Dad she wants to be a terrorist.

— The looks on their faces . . .

— She wants her own little room and a gun and a list of names.

— 'Targets.'

— A list – that's right – of so-called targets and their photographs. She wants to kill one a week then come back to the little room and drink Earl Grey tea.

— That's right – it has to be Earl Grey – and it has to be one a week.

— Her poor Mum and Dad are / *horrified*.

— They absolutely don't know how to take this.

— They've never bought Earl Grey tea / in their *lives*.

— She'd like to act like a machine, wouldn't she.

— Act? She'd like to *be* a machine. Sometimes she spends days on end, whole days on end pretending to be a television / or a car.

— A car or a television, an automatic pistol or a treadle sewing-machine.

Silence. In the silence:

> 'She is an excellent singles' host,
> and loves to take people
> on guided walks.'

— A sewing-machine . . . The things she comes out with . . .

— Then of course she's off round the world. One minute it's Africa, the next it's South America or Europe.

— Somewhere in Europe.

— Europe, Africa, South America, you name it. Brazil.

— Cuba. Brazil. Romania. / *Nigeria.*

— Romania. Cuba. Florida. Australia.

— That's right. Australia. New Zealand. The / Philippines.

— Morocco. Algeria. Tunisia. The Sahara Desert.

— The Kalahari Desert. The foothills of the Himalayas.

— The foothills of the Alps.

— That's right – the what's it called –

— The / Piedmont.

— The Piedmont, the Piedmont, the Piedmont, of course it is. Yes. Always some foothills somewhere with that big red bag of hers.

— And the same hair. Don't forget the same hair down /
to her waist.

— The same long hair down to her waist at forty as she
had at twenty – like a young girl still, isn't she, in
some of / those pictures.

— Even at forty she still looks and dresses like a young
girl half her age.

— But what's really conclusive is that the bag is full of
stones.

— The fascinating thing, that's right, is that the bag
turns out to be full / of stones.

— The stones are there to keep her under however much
she thrashes, and the handles of the bag are tied to
her ankles.

— No question in other words of a / cry for help.

— In other words she's planned all this, she's planned on
thrashing, she knew she'd thrash, and equally she
knew that the bag would go on dragging her down
regardless. So there's never at any point any question
of the attempt failing. There's never at any point any
question of anyone being able to intervene – not
Mum or Dad certainly.

— Well certainly not Mum and Dad – and certainly none
of her so-called *friends*.

— If you can *call* them / friends.

— Well you obviously *can't* call them friends.

Silence. In the silence:

> 'She likes to attend keep-fit classes,
> amateur dramatics, and take part
> in lively cabarets.

She is also a member of
her local rambling club.'

— And we're tempted to think – aren't we – that
perhaps the bag was *always* full of stones. From the
moment in fact that she left the house, her Mum and
Dad's house on her sixteenth birthday. Aren't we?

Pause.

Well aren't we?

— Aren't we what?

— Tempted. Tempted to imagine that maybe the bag was
always full of stones from that very first day. From
the moment she went down her Mum and Dad's path
and closed her Mum and Dad's gate and caught the
bus. That the red bag in the photographs is full of
stones. That on the trucks and trains and mules she
used to climb up mountains – and on the dumps and
slums and hillsides and cobbled renaissance piazzas,
the bag is full of stones. And in the refugee camps
where she posed at their request next to the stick-like
dying just as she posed apparently without a murmur
beside the Olympic swimming pools of paunchy
billionaires, the bag is full of stones. And on the airport
carousels. Particularly on the airport carousels at 2 a.m.
waiting with travellers from other time-zones and
war-zones for the machinery to start and the luggage
to appear through the black rubber curtain on the
black rubber track – the rucksacks and the leather
cases, the Samsonites and the taped-up cardboard
boxes – the bag, that red bag of hers is full of stones.

— We can't be sure.

— Well of course we can't be sure. But from what we
know of her, from what we see of her, it's not /
impossible.

— We can't be sure that the bag is full of stones. It could be full of old clothes, drugs . . . / anything.

— Why not? Why *can't* we be sure? Why can't we say once and for all that the bag is full of stones, and that the stones explain the smile.

— The stones, it's true, would explain the smile.

— The stones would definitely explain the smile from what we've seen of her. Because there is a funny side to this.

— A what?

— A side. A funny side.

— Oh yes. There's definitely a funny side.

Silence. In the silence:

> 'Ann feels that there is sometimes a problem with the word "singles", as it is often misunderstood. She would like to stress that these holidays are not match-making events, but instead bring like-minded people together in informal and friendly surroundings, allowing them to enjoy a holiday together, and leave as friends.'

7 THE NEW ANNY

Each speech is first spoken in an African or Eastern European language.* An English translation immediately follows.

— [phrase]
— The car twists along the Mediterranean road.

— [phrase]
— It hugs the bends between the picturesque hillside villages.

— [phrase]
— The sun gleams on the aerodynamic body.

— [phrase]
— The aerodynamic body of the new *Anny*.

— [phrase]
— We see the new *Anny* snake along between the red-tiled Mediterranean rooftops.

— [phrase]
— Fast.

— [phrase]
— Sleek.

— [phrase]
— Free.

— [phrase]
— We now understand that the *Anny* comes with electric windows as standard.

* In the first production, Serbo-Croatian.

— [phrase]
— We now understand that the *Anny* comes with driver's *and* passenger's airbag as standard.

— [phrase]
— We now understand that all the things other manufacturers offer as extras . . .

— [phrase]
— . . . are offered on the *Anny* as standard.

— [phrase]
— Air-conditioning.

— [phrase]
— Engine-immobiliser.

— [phrase]
— And a mobile telephone.

— [phrase]
— We understand that our children will be safe and happy in the back seat of the *Anny* just as the adults will be relaxed and confident at the wheel.

— [phrase]
— Happy.

— [phrase]
— Secure.

— [phrase]
— In control.

— [phrase]
— The *Anny* skims the white beaches of the world as easily as she parks outside the halogen-lit shoe shops of the great cities.

— [phrase]
— When we arrive at our destination in the *Anny* . . .

— [phrase]
— . . . we will always be embraced by good-looking
  men and good-looking women.

— [phrase]
— We will not be betrayed.

— [phrase]
— Tortured.

— [phrase]
— Or shot.

— [phrase]
— The two-litre *Anny* achieves excellent mileage in the
  simulated urban cycle . . .

— [phrase]
— . . . and is also available in diesel.

— [phrase]
— As a testimony to our ongoing concern for a cleaner,
  greener, environment . . .

— [phrase]
— . . . there are no filthy gypsies in the *Anny*.

— [phrase]
— Not in the *Anny* nor in the sun-filled landscapes
  through which the *Anny* drives.

— [phrase]
— No one in the *Anny* lies cheats or steals.

— [phrase]
— Dirty bastards.

— [phrase]
— Gangsters.

— [phrase]
— Motherfuckers.

— [phrase]
— There is no room in the *Anny* for the degenerate
  races . . .

— [phrase]
— . . . for the mentally deficient . . .

— [phrase]
— . . . or the physically imperfect.

— [phrase]
— No room for gypsies, Arabs, Jews, Turks, Kurds,
  Blacks or any of that human scum.

— [phrase]
— We understand that zero per cent finance is available.

— [phrase]
— But hurry.

— [phrase]
— Since this is a limited offer.

— [phrase]
— The *Anny* crosses the Brooklyn Bridge.

— [phrase]
— The *Anny* crosses the Sahara.

— [phrase]
— The *Anny* streaks through the vineyards of Bordeaux.

— [phrase]
— The *Anny* streaks at dawn through North African
  villages . . .

— [phrase]
— Fast.

— [phrase]
— Sleek.

— [phrase]
— Free.

— [phrase]
— . . . where the veiled women can only gaze with
    wonder at the immaculate rust-protected paintwork
    with its five-year warranty.

— [phrase]
— No one ever packs the *Anny* with explosives to
    achieve a political objective.

— [phrase]
— No man ever rapes and kills a woman in the *Anny*
    before tipping her body out at a red light along with
    the contents of the ashtray.

— [phrase]
— No one is ever dragged from the *Anny* by an enraged
    mob.

— [phrase]
— No child's pelvis is ever shattered by a chance
    collision with the new *Anny*.

— [phrase]
— The back seat is never made slippery by sperm.

— [phrase]
— Slippery by blood.

— [phrase]
— Slippery by beer.

— [phrase]
— Slippery by saliva.

— [phrase]
— Or sticky by melted chocolate.

— [phrase]
— Melted chocolate. Yum yum yum.

Small print:

— [phrase]
— On-the-road price includes VAT, number plates, delivery and six months' road fund licence.

— [phrase]
— Financial packages subject to status.

— [phrase]
— Smoking can harm your unborn child.

— [phrase]
— Your house is at risk if you do not keep up the repayments on a loan.

8 PARTICLE PHYSICS

— I'll tell you what: she has a kind of ashtray. The tall kind on a stalk. Like something you'd find in the lobby of a cheap hotel, the kind of hotel you visit for a few hours on a weekday afternoon in a strange city with a man you've / only just met.

— With a man you'll never see again.

— With a man – exactly – you've only just met and have no intention of ever seeing again. That's the kind of ashtray it is, with its chromium bowl and its chromium stalk and its aura of sudden unprotected sex in cheap hotel rooms.

— She also speaks five languages and with the aid of the CERN accelerator in Geneva has discovered a new elementary particle which will bear her name and completely change the way we look at the universe.

9 THE THREAT OF
INTERNATIONAL TERRORISM™

— She doesn't seem to care. She has no conscience. She
expresses no remorse. She says, 'I do not / recognise
your authority.'

— 'I do not recognise your authority.' Just what does she
mean by that? Who does she think she *is*? Does she
really imagine she won't have to account for the lives
she's destroyed? Does she really imagine that anything
can justify her acts of random senseless violence?
Nothing in her eyes reveals one spark / of human
feeling.

— Not one spark – that's right – of human feeling or any
sense of shame. Is this the same child, is this the same
child who once wore a pink gingham dress and a
straw hat and went with the daughters of doctors,
dentists, TV presenters and property developers to the
school on the hill with the polished brass plate and
the teachers in strict tartan skirts? Is this the same
child who had Fantasy Barbie™, Fantasy Ken™ and
all the outfits: the tiny tiny knickers and the tiny tiny
shoes? The house, the horse, and Barbie's™ / very
own car?

— Is this the same little Anne who put all the tiny tiny
shoes in rows and all the tiny tiny dolls in rows and
all the tiny tiny beads in rows and what's more
prayed to God™ each night / with no sense whatsoever
of irony.

— Who prayed to God™ 'God™ bless Mummy, God™
bless Daddy, God™ bless Wiggy the cat, God™ bless
everyone' with no sense whatsoever of irony but
rather in the sincere belief that she might invoke there
on her knees and in her Minnie Mouse™ pyjamas the
blessing of the Father and of the Son / and of the
Holy Ghost.

— Amen.

— Who wet the bed each and every night until her
sleepless parents took her to the doctor with his heap
of magazines to pull with a big smile down her
knickers on the high cold leather couch and say, 'Let's
take a look then, Anne, / shall we?'

— The same Anne who came away from the hospital
with a wooden box containing a bell to go beside the
bed, two stiff squares of metal gauze and a number /
of black wires?

— The same Anne who woke up each subsequent night
to the sound of the horrible bell in the horrible / wet
sheets?

— The same Anne who now – what? – *stands* there?
Stands there in front of serious men and women with
witnesses and evidence in sealed plastic bags – false
passports and pieces of human flesh – who stands
there and refuses / to recognise their *authority*?

— Pieces of human flesh, false passports, lists of names,
traces of explosive, tapes of phone-calls, videotapes
from banks and shopping malls and cash dispensers.
Psychiatric reports which confirm (a) her intelligence
and (b) her sanity. 'She set about her work,' they say,
'with all the terrible detachment of an artist.'
Witnesses break down / in tears.

— Witnesses break down in tears as videotapes from banks and shopping malls show Anne as just one more person going about their business under constant surveillance, until twenty minutes after she's left, the plate glass blows out of a shoe-shop window in absolute silence and the little grey figures breaking apart and flying through the air in absolute silence with the tiny tiny flying shoes are real human beings mixed with glass. No one can find out / what her motive is.

— No one can find Anne's motive.

— She lives alone?

— She lives alone.

— She works alone?

— She works alone.

— She sleeps alone?

— Apparently, yes.

— Kills / alone? Eats?

— She lives works sleeps kills and eats entirely on her own. In fact her recorded phone-calls consist almost entirely of orders for meals to be delivered to the rooms she rented overlooking the high streets of metropolitan suburbs – a large pizza, garlic bread, and one and a half litres of Diet Pepsi™ all for just nine pounds / ninety-nine.

— Calls which are at first assumed to be / coded messages.

— Calls which are at first, that's right, assumed to be coded messages but which are simply orders for meals delivered to her door by boys on scooters and / paid for in cash.

— Is this really the same little Anne who now has witnesses breaking down in tears? Who now has long-serving officers of both sexes receiving counselling for the night-sweats, impotence, amenorrhea, trembling hands and flashbacks of human heads popping open as if in slow motion and the long long terrible wail of a buried unreachable child recurring as a kind of what's the word?

— An auditory hallucination?

— Yes. For which they're now demanding / to be *compensated*.

— The same Anne who woke up when the bell went and watched the shadows of the chestnut trees move on her bedroom wall in her / wet pyjamas?

— The same Anne who soldered fiddly timing mechanisms and mercury tilt-switches to printed circuit boards with her mouth full of / deep-pan pizza?

— Who summed up the mood / of a generation.

— Who appeared twice on the cover of / *Vogue*™ magazine.

— Who sold the film rights for two and a half million / US dollars.

— Who studied in depth the baggage-handling procedures and memorised the timetables of the principal international / airlines.

— Who was quote a loner / unquote.

— Who listens quote expressionlessly unquote to the description of quote outrage unquote after quote outrage unquote after quote outrage unquote she has perpetrated.

10 KINDA FUNNY

— It's kinda funny and it's kinda sad.
I guess it's kinda bittersweet.
I guess it's one of these kinda bittersweet things, one
of these laughing through *tears* things.
After so much time, after so many years, he finally
comes back to his mom.
And at first, y'know, like 'Who *is* this?'
Then there's the moment of realisation: 'Oh *God*: it's
my very own son.'

And they're hugging each other right there in the
kitchen and y'know that is so *moving*.
I mean that is just so moving to see that he has found
that thing, that *strength,* to forgive his Mom.
That he has forgiven her her *alcoholism*.
That he has forgiven her for running round with
other *men*.
That he has forgiven her for destroying his father's
faith in himself and driving him to *suicide*.
And they're both kinda crying and laughing and
crying again all at the same time in the same kitchen
he sat in as a little boy witnessing his parents' terrible
arguments. His Dad in tears pouring her liquor down
the sink at ten o'clock in the morning while she
screams how if he was a real man with one iota of
self-respect she wouldn't need to booze herself to
death, would she. And there are these tiny scratches
in the table which he recalls having made secretly
with a fork. And you're aware, y'know, like of the
continuity of things, of the bittersweetness of things.

245

And then he says, 'Hey, Mom, I have a surprise for you.' And Mom kinda breaks away and wipes her eyes and says, 'What surprise?'

And he says, 'Look out the window, Mom.'
And out the window there's like this dusty pick-up with two tiny tiny kids in the back like kinda staring. Just staring into the camera.
And she can hardly believe these are her very own grandchildren.
Then he says, 'Mom, I want you to meet Annie.'

And that's when this woman Annie gets out of the pick-up and she's like real tall and fair and strong-limbed with these clear blue eyes that look right into your heart, and she's like – well I guess she's like every man's *dream* of what a good woman should be, and every mother's dream of the wife she would choose for her boy.

And it turns out how he and Annie and the kids are making this new what? Well, *life*. They are making this new, yes, life for themselves away from the city. Living off the land. Growing stuff. Trapping stuff. Boring under the earth for clean pure water. Educating their own *children*. In the belief that Man is free before God to forge his own destiny and take whatever means necessary to protect his family.

And over lunch – which is basically a kind of chicken salad with mayonnaise – we learn how he is in fact the commanding officer of a whole *group* of like-minded individuals who have armed themselves not out of any thirst for blood, but out of *necessity* because it is war. 'War?' says Mom. 'How d'you mean, war?'

So Annie has to explain to Mom how they don't believe in taxes or welfare or any of that shit. How

the war is a war against a government that takes the
bread out of the working man's mouth and gives it to
the pornographers and abortionists of this world.
Is a war against the God-forsaken *faggots*.
Is a war against the crack dealers and the Blacks.
Is a war against the conspiring *Jews* and their
attempts to rewrite *history*.
Is a *crusade* against the degenerate images which
masquerade as *art*.
Is a war against all those who would deny our right
to bear arms.

And Annie has like this inner light.
It's like wow, she's cut, she's cut, she's cut through all
the confusion and chattering voices of our lives and
of our time and found just this kinda really what?
Thing I guess.
This thing, this like absolute *thing*.
It's like she's found this thing.
It's like – hey – Annie has found this thing, this key,
yes, this key thing, this secret, this certainty and
simplicity, this secret and simple thing we all search
for throughout our lives and which is, I guess, the
truth.

Yes. And it's kinda moving to see how attentive *he* is
to the kids.
How he's the one who cuts up their chicken and
wipes their mouths with a paper napkin – the image,
y'know, of this big guy in camouflage doing all that
caring domestic stuff.
'Cos family is at the heart of things, I guess.

And one of the tiny tiny children looks up from his
chicken and says, 'Daddy, why is she *crying*?'
And it's true.
His mother is crying.

As she sits there at the family table gazing on this family she never knew she had – the son and his fine young wife, their strong and innocent children with their whole lives ahead of them – she is, yes indeed, crying her eyes out like a tiny child herself.

And Annie strokes the boy's hair – which is clipped real short, y'know – like a real young soldier – and says, 'Because she is so happy, son. Because she is so happy.'

11 UNTITLED (100 WORDS)

— What we see here are various objects associated with the artist's attempts to kill herself over the past few months. For example: medicine bottles, records of hospital admissions, Polaroids of the several HIV positive men with whom she has had intentionally unprotected intercourse, pieces of broken glass . . .

— Suicide notes.

— . . . yes, and the walls of the gallery have of course been lined with her many suicide notes. In addition to the Polaroids there are rather *unpleasant*, I have to say, video recordings of the attempts themselves.

Well I don't know about other people, but after a few minutes of this I rather began to wish she'd succeeded the first time round.

Silence. In the silence:

> head
> green
> water
> to sing
> death
> long
> ship
> to pay
> window
> friendly
> table
> to ask

cold

stem

to dance

village

lake

sick

pride

to cook

— Well I think that's an inexcusably frivolous comment to make about what is clearly a landmark work. It's moving. It's timely. It's distressing. It's funny. It's sick. It's sexy. It's deeply serious. It's entertaining. It's illuminating. It's dark. It's highly personal and at the same time raises vital questions about the world we're living in.

— What fascinates me is her use of textures. I think there's a great sensitivity here in the juxtaposition of materials: leather and glass, blood and paper, Vaseline and steel, which evoke in the viewer an almost / visceral reaction.

— I'm afraid what we're seeing here is pure narcissism. And I think we have to ask ourselves the question, who would possibly accept this kind of undigested exhibitionism as a work of art? . . .

— Yes, but exactly, that's surely the very point she's attempting to make: *Where* are the boundaries? *What* is acceptable? . . .

— . . . because it's pure / self-indulgence.

— . . . Where does the 'life' – literally in this case – end, and the 'work' begin?

— With respect to you I think she'd find the whole concept of 'making a point' ludicrously outmoded.

If *any* point is being made at all it's *surely* the point
that the point that's being made is *not* the point and
never has in fact *been* the point. It's surely the point
that a search for a point is pointless and that the whole
point of the exercise – i.e. these attempts on her own
life – *points* to that. It makes me think of the Chinese
proverb: the darkest place is always under the lamp.

Silence. In the silence:

ink
angry
needle
to swim
journey
blue
lamp
to sin
bread
rich
tree
to prick
pity
yellow
mountain
to die
salt
new
custom
to pray

— The what?

— The darkest place. It's / Chinese.

— *Why* can't people learn to draw? *Why* can't people
  learn to paint? Students should be taught *skills*, not
  ideas. Because what we see here is the work of a girl

who quite clearly should've been admitted not to an art school but to a psychiatric unit.

Silence. In the silence:

> money
> stupid
> exercise book
> to despise
> finger
> dear
> bird
> to fall
> book
> unjust
> frog
> to part
> hunger
> white
> child
> to pay attention
> pencil
> sad
> plum
> to marry

— *A what?*

— A mental hospital. Somewhere where she could / receive treatment.

— Well I have to say I think that's an extraordinary remark which I would not expect to hear outside of a police state . . .

— Oh *please* . . .

— . . . and which – no, I'm sorry, I'm sorry, this has to be said – which appears to be an attempt to reinstate the notion of *Entartete Kunst* . . .

— Oh rubbish. What an absurd / over-reaction.

— . . . the so-called 'degenerate art' prohibited – rubbish? I don't think so – prohibited by the Nazis. I mean *listen* to yourself: you are saying that this artist should not be allowed to produce work but should instead be compelled to undergo psychiatric treatment.

— I'm simply suggesting that this poor girl . . .

— 'This poor girl.'

— . . . this poor girl, yes, requires help – and I have not as you well know at any point suggested that she should be / 'compelled'.

— Requires help? Oh really? And in whose opinion? The opinion of Goebbels? The opinion perhaps of Joseph Stalin? Isn't Anne actually anticipating the terrifying consequences of that argument and asking us what 'help' actually means? Isn't she saying, 'I don't want your help'? Isn't she saying, 'Your help oppresses me'? Isn't she saying the only way to avoid being a victim of the patriarchal structures of late twentieth-century capitalism is to *become her own victim*?
Isn't that the true meaning of these attempts on her life?

— Her own victim – that's fascinating.

— Oh really, this is such flabby reasoning.

Silence. In the silence:

house
darling
glass
to quarrel
fur

big
carrot
to paint
part
old
flower
to beat
box
wild
family
to wash
cow
friend
happiness
to lie

— Well I think whatever the very varied personal
   agendas we bring to this, we're all agreed that it's
   a landmark work. It's moving. It's timely. It's
   distressing. It's funny. It's sick. It's sexy. / It's deeply
   serious. It's entertaining. It's cryptic. It's dark. It's
   highly personal and at the same time raises vital
   questions about the world we're living in.

— (*Cue 'sexy'*.) That really is such flabby reasoning. Her
   own victim? If she really is – as it appears – trying to
   kill herself, then surely our presence here makes us
   mere voyeurs in Bedlam. If on the other hand she's
   only play-acting, then the whole work becomes a
   mere cynical performance and is doubly disgusting.

— But why not? Why shouldn't it be / 'a performance'?

— Exactly – it becomes a kind / of theatre.

— It's theatre – that's right – for a world in which
   theatre itself has died. Instead of the outmoded
   conventions of dialogue and so-called characters

lumbering towards the embarrassing dénouements of the *theatre*, Anne is offering us a pure dialogue of objects: of leather and glass, of Vaseline and steel, of blood, saliva and chocolate. She's offering us no less than the spectacle of her own existence, the radical *pornography* – if I may use that overused word – of her own broken and abused – almost Christ-like – body.

— An object in other words. A *religious* object.

— An object, yes. But not the object of *others,* the object of *herself*. That's the scenario / she offers.

— But surely we've seen all that. Haven't we seen all that in the so-called 'radicalism' of the sixties stroke seventies?

Silence. In the silence:

> deportment
> narrow
> brother
> to fear
> stork
> false
> anxiety
> to kiss
> bride
> pure
> door
> to choose
> hay
> contented
> ridicule
> to sleep
> month
> nice

woman
to abuse

— *Seen* it – perhaps. But not seen it afresh, not seen it
now, not seen it in the context of a *post*-radical, of
a post-*human* world where the gestures of radicalism
take on new meaning in a society where the radical
gesture is simply one more form of entertainment i.e.
one more product – in this case an artwork – to / be
consumed.

— Theatre has nothing to do with this and I bitterly
resent the implication that I am some kind of a *Nazi*.

12 STRANGELY!

— She's driving away from the bombed-out city in a metallic red Cadillac circa 1956 . . .

— NAME!

— . . . when she reaches a checkpoint lit by burning tyres and is asked – exactly – for her name.

— STRANGELY!

— Strangely enough she doesn't reply to this reasonable request but begins instead a tirade of foul-mouthed abuse. 'You mother-fucking shit-faced murderers,' she says. 'You pig-fucking cock-sucking bastards.'

— LANGUAGE!

— 'You sister-fucking blaspheming child-murdering mindless fuck-faced killers.'

— LANGUAGE!

— 'I shit on your graves and on the graves of your mothers and fathers . . . '

— IDENTITY!

— '. . . and curse all future generations.' And then when asked once more – that's right – for her identity falls silent.

— SILENCE!

Silence.

WHAT?

Silence.

WHAT?

— Then she's mumbling something about her garden and the plum trees and the city's dried-up fountains. About – what's this? – the water she used to warm in plastic bottles so as not to shock the roots. She's mumbling something about . . .

— SPEAK UP!

— . . . she's mumbling something about – that's right: speak up you bitch – something about loss of electricity, nights spent in complete darkness and the decay of frozen meat. About the women banging saucepan lids in the streets as a kind of lamentation . . .

— NAME!

— . . . about the burning of entire libraries full of books and irreplaceable manuscripts and about stale bread thrown off the back of trucks and on and on about the plums and the white flowers . . .

— MEANWHILE!

— . . . and the smell of sewage coffee and human remains and meanwhile – that's right: meanwhile – thank you – the soldiers crowd round this nameless woman with the long grey hair streaked with blood and round the red Cadillac lit by the stacks of burning tyres and ask her just where the fuck, where the fuck on this Godforfuckingsaken earth does she think she's going?

Silence.

— WHAT?

Silence.

— WHAT?

— 'The airport.'

— SPEAK UP!

— 'The airport. I'm taking my child to the airport. You don't have to shout at me. I'm an educated woman – not some peasant out of a field who came to the city to clean rich people's toilets. I have a passport and a bank account in US dollars and I'm taking my child to the airport.'

— STRANGELY!

— 'Now please let me pass.' But yes, as you say, strangely there is no child to be seen. Child? What child? And women with passports don't look like this. Women with US dollars don't look like this. Their hair is streaked professionally in salons with artificial highlights, not with human blood. They don't drive battered Cadillacs, they own four-wheel-drive Japanese jeeps with a spare tyre they will never use strapped to the rear door. Let's shine a flashlight, shall we, on to the back seat and see just what she's talking about.

— CHILD? WHAT CHILD?

— Let's get out the rubber – what child – exactly – flashlight, and see just what it is she's talking about, just what it is she means by 'child', this nameless woman with the long grey hair and nastily pock-marked face. And while we're on the subject of her appearance, why can't she be more attractive? Why can't she be more sympathetic? Why can't she have a few more teeth? Why can't she bend over and let us see her ass? Why can't she break down in tears and make us long to comfort her instead of staring like that and spitting.

— STRANGELY!

— So – what? – yes – sorry – strangely as you say the
light from the torch reveals on the back seat of the
vehicle only two shiny black plastic bags each tied at
the neck but no child whatsoever.

— CHILD? WHAT CHILD?

— And now she's mumbling something about . . .

— SPEAK UP!

— . . . something about a garden swing, something
about her little girl, her little Anne, her little
Annushka. Something – what's this? Speak up –
something about her Annushka 'being in the bags'
and about her need, her urgent need to take these
bags to the airport with her education and her bank
account in US dollars and buy air tickets.
Doesn't she realise the airport is closed?
Didn't she hear the runway being bombed?
Didn't she see the intelligent rockets splash up the
concrete like stones dropped into a pool?

— STRANGELY!

— Can't she feel the white heat of the burning aviation
fuel? No. Strangely as you say she seems to believe
the airport is functioning normally. Strangely she
seems to think that the world's white beaches and
cosmopolitan cities are still a few hours away by
regular scheduled flights.

— STRANGELY!

— This nameless woman strangely seems to imagine she
can still operate a bank account with a plastic card
and fly first class with little Anne, with Annushka,
out of the range of rifles and axes, to a city full of

art galleries, halogen lamps, charming cafés and
attractively displayed shoes.

— STRANGELY!

Silence.

— And yes – strangely – no one asks her what she means
by Annushka 'being in the bags'.

— STRANGELY!

Silence.

— And yes – strangely – no one asks to examine the
bags.

— STRANGELY!

Silence.

— And yes – most strangely perhaps of all – no one
questions why a child should be in two bags as
opposed to one.

Silence.

— STRANGELY!

13 COMMUNICATING WITH ALIENS

— *Then* we discover that she is being penetrated by mysterious rays which make her invisible in photographs.

— What? X-rays?

— No, not X-rays. It's a new kind of ray. It's a new kind of ray produced by a catastrophe in *deep / space*.

— You mean – okay – that she is in communication are you saying via these rays with *aliens*?

— Not *communication*. No. The aliens are *using* her. They are using her, but *without her / knowledge*.

— The aliens – that's right – are using her mind as a kind of Trojan Horse by which they can gradually invade all of human / *consciousness*.

— And the frightening thing is, is she could be any one of us.

14 GIRL NEXT DOOR

She's the girl next door
She's the fatal flaw
She's the reason for
The Trojan War.

She is royalty
She practises art
She's a refugee
In a horse and cart.

She's a pornographic movie star
A killer and a brand of car
A KILLER AND A BRAND OF CAR!

She's a terrorist threat
She's a mother of three
She's a cheap cigarette
She is Ecstasy.

She's a femme fatale
She's the edge of the knife
She's one helluva gal
She's Intelligent Life.

She's a presidential candidate
For every little warring state
EVERY LITTLE WARRING STATE!

She winters in the south
She collects antiques

She has a big mouth
But she never speaks.

She's given a spade
At the edge of a wood
To dig her own grave
By a man in a hood.

She drives a tank
Over neonates
While choosing to bank
At competitive rates.

She bombs by stealth
Has unlimited wealth
White knobbly knees.
WHAT? KNOBBLY KNEES?
Yes. Knobbly knees
And speaks fluent Japanese.

O-shigoto wa nan desu ka?
Oku-san wa imasu ka?
OKU-SAN WA IMASU KA?

She's an artificial tan
She's the fat in the pan
She's the film in the can
She's the shit in the fan.

She's the one who ran
When the shooting began.

She's a girl with a plan
She's a boy with a man
She's a dyke with a *femme*
She's a man with a van.

She's a dedicated football fan
With limited attention span
LIMITED ATTENTION SPAN!

She's the predator
She's the god of war
She's the fatal flaw

She's the girl she's the girl
She's the girl she's the girl
She's the girl she's the girl
SHE'S THE GIRL NEXT DOOR!

15 THE STATEMENT

Silence.

— You say she rides her bike in all weathers?

— All weathers. That's right.

Silence.

— And wears a hat.

— Yes. She wears a hat.

— Which, you state, she has knitted herself.

— I believe so.

Silence.

— She grows tomato plants in . . .

— Margarine tubs.

— Margarine tubs.

— That's right.

Silence.

Or yoghurt . . .

— Yoghurt pots.

— Yes.

— I see.

Silence.

Why do you think she does that?

— What? Grow tomato plants?

— Yes.

Silence.

— For fêtes.

— For what?

— Fêtes. She sells them at fêtes.

— Of course. And I suppose she takes them to the fêtes on her bike.

— Yes she does.

— In all weathers.

— Yes she does.

— In a cardboard box.

— Yes she does.

— Now why do you suppose she does that? Why do you suppose she takes these, what, these tomato plants in yoghurt pots, why do you suppose she takes them on her bike in a cardboard box to fêtes in all weathers?

Long silence.

You state quote as a child she often shared a bed with two or three of her younger siblings unquote. Do you abide by that statement?

— Yes.

— Why?

— Because she did.

— 'Because she did.'

— Because she did, yes. Because they were poor. Because they had nothing.

— Different world, eh?

Silence.

If you could just sign here.

— What?

— Yes. If you could just sign here to say you have read the statement, and consider it accurate.

Silence.

Well, don't you consider it accurate?

— If I could have a pen . . .

A pen is produced, the cap removed. The paper is signed and passed back.

Silence.

Is that all?

— For the time being. Thank you.

Silence.

Thank you very much.

Silence.

16 PORNÓ

*The principal speaker is a very young woman. As she speaks her words are translated dispassionately into an African, South American or Eastern European language.**

— The best years of her life are ahead of her.
— [translation]

— She may be seventeen or eighteen . . .
— [translation]

— . . . but ideally she's younger . . .
— [translation]

— . . . fourteen perhaps or younger still.
— [translation]

— It's really really important to understand that she is in control.
— [translation]

— She's always in control of everything that happens.
— [translation]

— Even when it looks violent or dangerous.
— [translation]

— Which it is not.
— [translation]

— (*faint laugh*) Obviously.
— [translation]

* In the first production, Portuguese as spoken in Brazil.

— (*faint laugh*) Of course there's no *story* to speak of . . .
— [translation]

— . . . or characters.
— [translation]

— Certainly not in the conventional sense.
— [translation]

— But that's not to say that skill isn't required.
— [translation]

— Since we still need to feel that what we're seeing is real.
— [translation]

— It isn't just acting.
— [translation]

— It's actually far more exacting than acting – for the simple reason that it's really happening.
— [translation]

A pause. She seems to have forgotten what to say and looks for a prompt.

— Yes?

— (*prompt*) She enjoys her work.
— What?
— (*more emphatic prompt*) She enjoys her work.
— She enjoys her work.
— [translation]

— She's young and fit, and happy with her body.
— [translation]

— How she uses her body is her decision.
— [translation]

— Obviously.
— [translation]

— Porno doesn't stop her leading a normal life.
— [translation] (*In the translation 'Porno' should have a distinctive stress: 'Pornó'.*)

— She has a regular boyfriend . . .
— [translation]

— . . . and all the normal interests of a girl of her age.
— [translation]

— (*faint laugh*) Clothes.
— [translation]

— Boys.
— [translation]

— Make-up. Pets.
— [translation]

— Music.
— [translation]

— The difference is . . .
— [translation]

— . . . is that Porno is building up for her the kind of security and independence many women would envy.
— [translation]

— Porno.
— [translation]

— . . . is actually a way of taking control.
— [translation]

— Porno . . .
— [translation]

— . . . is actually the reverse of what it seems.
— [translation]

— Because rather than *consuming* the images . . .
— [translation]

— . . . she is producing them.
— [translation]

— That, for her, is one of the beauties of Porno.
— [translation]

Again a pause. She seems to have forgotten what to say: but this should imply a distress which is never allowed to surface. She looks for a prompt.

— Yes?
— (*prompt*) She is not insensitive to the evening light.
— What?
— (*more emphatic prompt*) She is not insensitive / to the evening light.
— She is not insensitive to the evening light when it strikes the tops of the pine trees with brilliant orange.
— [translation]

— She has an inner life.
— [translation]

— She responds sensitively to the world.
— [translation]

— The scenario in fact of the drugged and desensitised child . . .
— [translation]

— . . . humiliated . . .
— [translation]

— . . . and then photographed or filmed without her knowledge . . .
— [translation]

— . . . is a ludicrous caricature.
— [translation]

Again a pause. Again she looks for a prompt.

— Yes?
— (*prompt*) Everything is provided.
— What?
— (*more emphatic prompt*) Everything is provided for her needs.

Pause.

— I can't.
— [translation of 'I can't']

Pause.

— I can't.
— [translation of 'I can't']

She turns away. Momentary confusion. But then another speaker takes over. In fact the rest of the company have probably appeared and may share the following lines, while the first girl drinks a glass of water and is revived; again it should not be clear whether she's suffering stage fright or true distress.

The translator remains impassive.

— Everything is provided for her needs. Including a regular education.
— [translation]

— By age twenty-one the best years of her life will still be ahead of her . . .
— [translation]

— . . . *and* she'll have money in the bank from Porno.
— [translation]

— Not everyone has this start in life.
— [translation]

— Or her opportunities.
— [translation]

— Obviously.
— [translation]

The young woman gradually begins to join in again, supported by the other voices.

— She could for example become a model . . .
— [translation]

— . . . a TV personality . . .
— [translation]

— . . . run her own country pub or travel the world.
— [translation]

— She could paint . . .
— [translation]

— . . . swim professionally . . .
— [translation]

— . . . or study for a degree in chemical engineering.
— [translation]

All with growing élan.

— Anne could change the world . . .
— [translation]

— . . . end animal suffering . . .
— [translation]

— . . . end human suffering . . .
— [translation]

— . . . and learn to fly helicopters.
— [translation]

Passionate gypsy violin music begins.

— Anne will distribute the world's resources evenly across the earth . . .
— [translation]

— . . . raise from the dust the faces of the disaffected . . .
— [translation]

— . . . while guaranteeing not to erode the privileges of the middle class.
— [translation]

— She will popularise psychoanalytic theory . . .
— [translation]

— . . . by probing the roots of human behaviour . . .
— [translation]

— . . . in a series of weekly magazine articles.
— [translation]

The music intensifies.

— Anne has seen the world from space . . .
— [translation]

— . . . the wrinkles of the mountains . . .
— [translation]

— . . . and the cobalt threads of the rivers.
— [translation]

— She has excavated the shallow graves . . .
— [translation]

— . . . and picked over the shattered skulls of the dead.
— [translation]

— She has scattered information in the optic fibres . . .
— [translation]

— . . . and danced with the particles of light.
— [translation]

Music intensifies. The speakers divide, creating two simultaneous strands, each strand impassively translated into a different language:

— Anne has hosed down the
streets of Bucharest
— [translation]
— . . . and listened to the
foetal heart.
— [translation]
— She has melted with the
ice-caps . . .
— [translation]
— . . . and flowed into
the fertile deltas.
— [translation]

— She has personally
endorsed a brand of
imported lager.
— [translation]

— She has bought an entire
newspaper page . . .
— [translation]
— . . . to print a full and
unreserved apology.
[translation]

— She has exterminated
gypsies . . .
— [translation]

— . . . and bought a sprig
of lucky heather.
— [translation]

— Anne will now demonstrate
the crash position . . .
— [translation]

— . . . which you should
adopt when instructed by
the stewards . . .
— [translation]

— Head down.
— [translation]

— Knees drawn up.
— [translation]

— If oxygen is required . . .
— [translation]

— . . . oxygen masks will
drop down automatically.
— [translation]

— Pull on the mask to start
the oxygen.
— [translation]

— Do not smoke while
oxygen is in use.
— [translation]

— Please ensure that your
seat-belt is fastened . . .
— [translation]

— . . . your table is folded

276

— She has hung on a
cross to die . . .
— [translation]

— . . . risen on the third
day from the dead . . .
— [translation]

— . . . grown a beard . . .
[translation]

— . . . and entered
Mecca in triumph.
— [translation]

— Anne will save us from
the anxiety of our
century . . .
— [translation]

— . . . and usher in an
age in which the
spiritual and the
material . . .
— [translation]

— . . . the commercial
and the trivial . . .
— [translation

— . . . the wave and the
particle . . .
— [translation]

— . . . will finally be
reconciled!
— [translation]

away . . .
— [translation]

— and that your seat is
in an upright position.
— [translation]

— During the flight . . .
— [translation]

— . . . we will be coming round
with a list of duty-free
goods.
— [translation]

— Anne will save us from the
anxiety of our century . . .
— [translation]

— . . . and usher in an age
in which the spiritual and
the material . . .
— [translation]

— . . . the commercial and
the trivial . . .
— [translation]

— . . . the wave and the
particle . . .
— [translation]

— . . . will finally be reconciled!
— [translation]

277

— Okay, so there's a lot on her mind. Things have . . .

— Well that's right.

— . . . things have what? Things have *changed* for her over the past few years.

— Well that's absolutely right.

— I mean we can see – let's face it: we can see that something has died.

— Something has what?

— Has died. Something / has died.

— She feels she's failed.

— Exactly. She feels her work's failed.

— But also personally – her work, yes – but also personally she feels that something, something inside of her has died.

— And *has* it?

— What?

— And *has* it died?

— Has what died?

— This thing, this so-called thing inside of her.

— What so-called thing?

— The thing, the thing, the thing, the thing / inside of her.

— In her case, yes, let's say it *has* died. Let's say that everything she's ever worked for – her whole life – has died. (*laughter*) Let's say her life up to this point has been what? what? what? like a . . .

— Book?

— Like a book, like a . . .

— Thread?

— Like a book, like a thread, like a . . .

— Boat?

— Like a boat. Let's say her whole life – yes, very good – up to this point has been like a boat, like a small boat . . .

— Drifting.

— . . . drifting quite happily across a lake. But now she feels the water . . .

— Coming in through the cracks?

— Creeping.

— Creeping into what?

— Her broken heart.

Laughter.

— Her broken – exactly – yes – absolutely – heart. She feels the water of the lake creeping into her / broken heart.

— Her *work* abandoned. Her *home* abandoned by her children.

— Her*self* abandoned by her *husband*. Where is *he* now?

— Paris? Prague? / Vienna? Berlin?

— Paris? Prague? Fucking? Fucking is he someone half her age in a city of Renaissance palaces and baroque / domes? Enacting some adolescent fantasy, while she attempts to reconstruct her life.

— But she never had a husband.

— She never what?

— Never had a husband. She never believed in marriage.

— Okay. Perhaps she never believed in it, but she had a husband all the same.

Laughter.

— Paul.

— Who?

— Paul.

— Paul? Paul wasn't her *husband*.

Laughter.

— Well who was he then?

— I don't know. He was just some kind of, some kind of, some kind of . . . / person.

— Like smoking.

— What? Exactly. Yes. Like smoking cigarettes.

Silence.

— Talking of which, d'you know she still has that tall ashtray on a stalk?

— Talking of what?

— Of which. Talking of which.

— She doesn't.

— She does. She still carries it round with her from / room to room.

— It's a ghastly thing.

— It is not a ghastly thing.

— It's like something out of the lobby of a cheap hotel, the kind of hotel you visit for a few hours on a weekday afternoon in a strange city with a man you've / only just met.

— It is. It's like a *spittoon*. Or what's that other thing?

— What thing is that?

— That thing. That word. That other word.

— With a man you'll never see again.

— What? For spittoon?

— With a man – exactly – you've only just met and have no intention of ever seeing again. With its chromium bowl and its chromium stalk and its aura of sudden unpro-tected sex in cheap hotel rooms. A cuspidor? What's that?

— Humidor?

— No. Not humidor, but like it.

Pause.

— Cuspidor?

— Cuspidor. That's it. It's like a cuspidor.

— A thing. A thing you spit in.

— She doesn't spit. What are you talking about? She doesn't marry. She doesn't have children. And she certainly / doesn't spit.

— No one's saying she spits.

— So why then does she have a thing you spit in?

— She doesn't have a thing you spit in, she has a thing that / *resembles* one.

— But in that case, what's a humidor?

— Humidor is Spanish. Like matador.

— Like conquistador.

— It's a box where you / keep cigars.

— It's a box – that's right – where you keep cigars.

Silence.

— So. What? She doesn't work?

— She *does* work.

— She *has* worked.

— She *can* work.

— She *will* work.

— She *won't* work.

— What?

— She won't work.

— But she has skills.

— Oh yes, she has skills but whatever skills she has seem inappropriate to the world she's living in. Whatever work she's done seems inappropriate to the world she's living in. All she can do is pace round the ashtray or pull down books at random from the bookshelves.

— Don't tell me: classic texts.

— That's right – the classic texts she should've read as a student twenty or thirty years ago.

— And just like twenty or thirty years ago gets no
further than the introductions.

Laughter.

— The bits she underlined with a shaky black biro . . .

— Those bits – exactly – that she underlined in biro
because she thought they had some what? Some
meaning?

— Or was taught.

— Or was what?

— Taught. Not necessarily thought, but taught. Taught
they had / some meaning.

— Well – thought, taught, whatever, the fact remains
she'd rather skim.

— Okay, you mean to skim seems more appropriate to
the world / she's living in?

— That's exactly what I mean: she'd rather skim. She'd
rather read just the smallest parts of things. Part of
a recipe. Part of a letter. Part of / an article.

— Part of a recipe. Part of a letter replying to a letter
she's never read about an article she missed.

— What article was that?

— She missed it.

— She missed it – okay – but we can still imagine what
she might've missed.

— That thing about the actor.

— That thing about the politician.

— That thing about the fresh salmon.

— That thing about the killer. How he'd inflicted a total of 37 stab-wounds on the child's mother as the child slept.

— What thing was that?

— The salmon?

— And it was his own child.

— Yes.

— No, it wasn't his own child. But his own child was there.

— Well about how you define the word 'fresh'. What the word 'fresh' in a phrase like 'fresh salmon' actually means.

— He brought his child to watch.

— He brought his own child – that's right – to watch him murder this other child's mother.

— You mean can it mean 'previously frozen'?

— Exactly.
He did *what*?

— Brought his own child. Brought his own child in his pyjamas to watch him do it. Stab her. Yes.

Silence.

— And *can* it?

— Can it what?

— Mean 'previously frozen'?

Silence.

THE COUNTRY

The Country was first performed at the Royal Court
Theatre, London, on 11 April 2000. The cast in order
of appearance was as follows:

Richard Owen Teale
Corinne Juliet Stevenson
Rebecca Indira Varma

Director Katie Mitchell
Designer Vicki Mortimer
Lighting Designer Paule Constable
Sound Designer Gareth Fry
Movement Director Struan Leslie
Dialect Coach Jeannette Nelson
Company Voice Work Patsy Rodenburg

Characters

Corinne
forty

Richard
forty

Rebecca
twenty-five

Corinne and Richard are from London

Rebecca is American

Time
The present

Place
The country

I

Interior. Night.
  A large room, wooden chairs, an old table.
  Richard and Corinne.

—What are you doing?

—I'm cutting.

—What are you cutting?

—I don't know . . . I'm making something. Why are you
  looking at me like that?

—You don't normally cut. You don't normally make
  things. What are you making?

—I just thought I'd cut out some pictures to go round
  the cot. I thought they'd be stimulating.

—Are they bright?

—Some of them are bright.

  She cuts.

  Some of them are just pictures.

—It's a good idea.

—D'you think it's a good idea? I'm not sure if it's a
  good idea.

—Have you got enough light?

—Oh, I've got plenty of light. Thank you.

  She cuts.

This . . . . person. Is she asleep? When will she wake up?

—Don't hurt your eyes.

—Is she alive?

—Well of course she's alive. What sort of question / is that?

—Well I don't know, do I? I don't know if she's alive.

—Of course she's alive. She's asleep.

—Did you give her something?

—Something what?

—Something to make her.

—Not to make her but to help her.

—Not to make her but to help her. Is there a difference?

—No.

Both faint laugh.

—Because why did you bring her here? Why ever did you bring her here?

—It's my job to bring her here.

—What? Into our house? In the middle of the night?

—Yes.

—Is it?

—Yes.

—Your *job*? It's your job to bring a strange woman into our house in the middle of the night?

—As I understand it.

—And *what* was she doing?

—I've told you what she was doing.

Pause.

D'you want something to drink?

—Lying there.

—Yes. Do you?

—Lying on the road.

—She was next to it.

—What? Sprawled? Sprawled next to it?

—(*shrugs*) If you like.

—Partying then.

—What?

—She'd been partying.

—I've no idea. She was incoherent.

—What? Completely incoherent? What sort of party was it? I'm glad she's not mine.

—Your what?

—My child. I'm glad she's not my child.

—She's not a child.

—Someone must love her, though.

—Why?

—Someone must.

He moves to go out.

I don't want alcohol.

—I'll get you some water.

He goes out.
She cuts.

—Have you called Morris?

—(*off*) What?

—Have you called Morris? Shouldn't he be informed?

—(*off*) Morris?

—Shouldn't you inform him?

—(*off*) He'll be asleep.

—D'you think he sleeps, then?

—(*off*) What?

He reappears with glass of water.

What?

—I can't imagine Morris asleep. (*Takes water.*) Thank you. I imagine him . . . alert, somehow. Permanently alert.

She sips.

—D'you think I should call him?

—It's just that you don't seem concerned.

—Well that's my job.

—Your job is not to be concerned?

—My job is not to seem it.

—Taste this.

—What?

—Taste it.

He sips the water.

—I can't taste anything.

—But there's a taste of something.

—What?

—Something . . . I don't know . . . purity. D'you think it's safe?

—It's water, that's all. It's a glass of water.

—But shouldn't there be something in it?

—It's just a glass of water.

—That's what I'm saying.

—It's water – it's pure – and so perhaps it has a taste.

—You can taste it then?

—I can't taste anything. It has no taste. It tastes of nothing. But perhaps that taste of nothing is what you can taste.

—You can't then?

—No, I can't. I'm sorry.

—You drink it.

—Don't you want it?

—No. You drink it.

He drinks all the water.
Pause.
She begins to laugh.

—What is it?

—The look on your face.

—What look on my face?

—When you appeared. The look on your face when you appeared with her in your arms.

—Oh? What was I doing?

—Smiling.

—What at?

—Well that's just it: you were standing there with this girl in your arms, smiling. And I thought: oh look, he's lost his sense of humour. He's finally lost his famous sense / of humour.

—But in fact you were wrong.

—In fact I was wrong.

—In fact my famous sense of humour survives intact.

—In fact your famous sense of humour does – yes – survive / intact.

—Because I think you should tell me. I think you should tell me if you feel I've done something wrong.

—No no no, what you've . . .

—Thank you.

—What you've . . . Wrong? No. Of course not.

—Thank you. / Good.

—What you've done is . . . What you've done is exactly what someone *would have done*.

—People can't be left.

—Well that's right.

—Can they?

—I don't think that they *can*, no. Clearly they *can't*.

—This isn't the city.

—I know.

—This isn't the city, you can't just . . .

—I know you can't.

Pause.

So there wasn't a bag?

—A what?

—A bag. A purse. Didn't she have some kind of . . .

—A purse?

—Yes. A purse. A bag. Whatever. Don't look so / blank.

—Why do you say that: purse?

—Why do I say it?

—Yes. Why do you say it when it's not English?

—What is not English?

—Purse is not English.

—I'm not speaking English?

—Of course you're speaking / English.

—Well did she?

—What? Sorry?

—Have one.

—Have a bag?

—Did she?

—I'm not . . .

—You're not sure.

297

—No.

—You didn't . . .

—No.

—You didn't look.

—No. For a bag? No. Why?

—'Why?'

—Yes.

—What?

Pause.

What? Because if there was a bag . . .

—I know.

—If there was a bag . . .

—Yes – only the light was going . . .

— . . . then we could look – couldn't we – in the bag and it might . . . / simplify things. We wouldn't be . . .

—I've told you: the light was going. The imperative was to get her off that road and to ensure her safety. The bag was not – yes, it would simplify things – but the bag was not, as I'm sure you can imagine, uppermost in my mind.

—The bag.

—What?

—So there was a bag.

—I don't know if there was a bag.

—If there was a bag, you should go back. You should go back and look for it.

—D'you want me to go back and look for it? If you want me to go back and look for it, I'll go back and look for it.

—No, I don't want you to go back and look for it, I want you to kiss me.

—I don't want to kiss you. I *have* kissed you.

—Then kiss me again.

—I don't want to kiss you again.

—Why? Don't you love me?

Pause.

—What?

—You don't have to look so blank. I said: don't you / love me?

—I don't want to kiss you. I don't feel clean.

—Well you look clean.

—I don't feel it.

—Then take a shower. Take a shower, and when you're clean come back and kiss me.

—I'll wake the children up.

—I don't think you will wake the children up.

—How have they been?

—Oh, sweet.

Pause.

I took them to Sophie's, actually. I left them at Sophie's for the afternoon. I had a whole afternoon free. Sophie's so kind.

—I hope you gave her something.

—I always give her something. In fact I always give her
far too much. As if she were poor.

—She is poor.

—Sophie? I didn't know she was poor.

—Everyone knows she's poor.

—But she's so neat. And her house is so neat. It's so
clean. She has flowers in the kitchen. What d'you
mean, 'she's poor'?

—She has no money.

—She has a house.

—The house is collapsing. It isn't hers. She's a tenant.

—I don't believe you. I don't believe Sophie's poor. She
can't be.

—That cup she puts the money in? Well all the money
she has at any time is in that cup.

Pause.

—Well don't you want to hear what I did with my
afternoon?

Pause.

I'll tell you what I did, then.

—What did you do?

—I took one of these old chairs and I sat under a tree.

—That sounds nice.

—It was lovely.

Pause.

—Which tree was that?

—The one by the stream.

—The alder.

—Is that the alder?

—The one by the stream / is, yes.

—Well whatever it is, I sat under it. Sat under it for so
long in fact that the back legs sank into the moss. And
I just looked at the land. I sat there and I just looked
out at the land.

Pause.

—And how was the land?

—It was lovely. The land was lovely. All the hills were
rolling and all the clouds were unravelling, like in a
fairy tale. I felt like that girl in the fairy tale. Who's
that girl in the fairy tale?

—A goat-girl.

—A goat-girl or something. I felt – that's right – just like
a goat-girl, only without the goats thankfully. And I
thought of you driving, with your sense of humour,
which I felt sure you would need, along all those
country lanes to visit the sick and so on, and I can't
tell you how happy I felt, how good it all felt. Which
is when Morris appeared.

—What did *Morris* want?

—Well that's what *I* said. I said, 'What can I do for you,
Morry?' He said, 'I see you're making yourself quite
at home.' I said, 'Well this *is* my home now, Morry.'
He said, 'I'm sorry if I'm disturbing you, I was
looking for Richard.' I said, 'Richard's not here,

I'm afraid. Presumably he's out doing the rounds.'
And Morris said, 'Yes. That must be it.'

Pause.

—I hope you were nice to him.

—I was incredibly nice to him. Even when he squatted right next to me in his terrible tweeds.

—Oh God, not the terrible tweeds.

—He squatted right next to me – yes – and asked how we were settling in.

—What did he mean by that?

—He just asked how we were settling in. Did we miss the city?

—And did we?

—What? Miss the city? Well *I* didn't. I told him I couldn't speak for you.

—Did he expect you to speak for me?

—I don't know what he expected. He said he was on his way to the DIY superstore to buy some paint, and did we need anything?

—Paint?

—Yes. Apparently he has little posts lining his driveway and every year he paints them.

—Doesn't he have any paint at home?

—Well that's what I said. I said, 'Don't you have any paint at home?' And no, he doesn't. Or rather, yes, he does. He does have some paint at home – it's the paint he used last time he painted the posts – only he doesn't know where it is.

Pause.

—So someone's moved the pot.

—No, he thinks he's moved the pot himself. He feels sure he moved the pot, but he doesn't remember where. I said, 'That must be very frustrating for you, Morry.' But the thing is, is then he began to talk to me in another language. One moment it was English – the paint and so on – then the next it was like he was chanting to me in another language. I said, 'What's that, Morry?' And of course I couldn't help laughing. He said, 'It's Latin. It's Virgil.'

—Virgil.

—Well that's what *I* said. I said, '*Virgil*, Morris? You make me feel so ignorant.' And he did. He was making me feel very very ignorant. Squatting there. Chanting like that.

—Surely not. Surely he meant well.

—Well no, I don't think that he did. I don't think that he did 'mean well'. I kept thinking, 'Why have you come here? What do you want?'

—And what *did* he want?

—Well that's what I kept wondering. He said it was about bees. That seeing me sitting like that next to a stream brought it back to him.

—Brought what back to him?

—This thing. This . . . poem.

—Christ.

—Yes. And it's just that I can't help thinking, what if it had been a man? (*faint laugh*) Don't look so blank.

303

I'm just wondering – if it – she – if she had been a
man, would you have been so . . . (*shrugs*) That's all.

—A man.

—Would you still have been so – a man, yes – so
solicitous?

—'Would I still have been so solicitous?'

—Well *would* you? *Would* you – if instead of . . .

—Solicitous.

—Yes. If instead of some frail young . . . slim young . . .
abandoned at the / side of a road.

—What d'you mean, / 'solicitous'?

—If instead of this . . . vision, this victim of some
unspecified, some undiagnosed . . . misfortune, let's
say it had been some man you had found, some man
perhaps crawling out of a ditch with his clothes
covered in muck . . .

—No one – I'm sorry – but no one was crawling / out of
any ditch.

—Well all right then – not crawling, but unconscious.
You round the bend and instead of that, that . . .
person, it's a man who's drunk himself into a stupor
and he's lying there in his own sick and he's wet
himself. Would you really have lifted this man into
your car? Would you have driven him all this way to
your own house where your children are sleeping?

She resumes cutting.

That's all I meant by solicitous.

—I can't help what sex she is.

—Well obviously.

—And besides, she hasn't been sick. She hasn't wet herself.

—So far as you know.

—So far as I know.

—*Do you know?*

—What?

—*Do you know?*

She accidentally cuts herself with the scissors – sucks her finger – looks at him.

—Well yes, it's my job, isn't it, as a matter of fact, to know.
    What have you done?

—Oh. Nothing. Cut myself.

—Is it deep? Does it hurt? Wash it.

—I'd rather suck it.

—Well suck it then.

They both laugh.
    He moves away.

—Where are you going?

—I'm going to take that shower. He goes out.

She squeezes her finger, looks at the blood.

(. . . scissors)

II

The same scene, a few minutes later.
  Corinne, alone, has a small object pressed to her ear.
  Richard appears, doing up his shirt, watching her.
  She dangles the object – a wristwatch – by its thin gold bracelet, and smiles to herself.

—Why did you do that?

—It's her watch.

—I know it's her watch. Give it to me, please.

—To you?

—Yes.

  She closes it in her fist.
    They both smile.

—I wanted to touch her.

—Why did you want to touch her?

—To see if she was hot.

—And was she?

—What?

—Hot.

—I uncovered her.

—You're not to uncover her.

  Pause.

  Why did you uncover her?

—I was curious about her arms, actually. Have you looked at her arms?

—No, I haven't looked at her arms.

—Her legs, then. Have you looked at her face? Haven't you looked at her? Haven't you looked at any part of her?

Pause.

Aren't you curious?

—I'd like you to give me the watch. I'd like you to stop clutching it. Why are you clutching it like that?

—I'm not clutching it, I'm holding it in my hand.

—You'll damage it.

Pause.
She holds the watch out to him.

—It's beautiful. It shows the phases of the moon.

As he gets close and reaches for the watch, she snaps it back in her fist.

—But first you have to kiss me.

—I have kissed you.

—Then you have to kiss me again.

She slowly opens her fist. He comes closer, he takes the watch, she grips his hand, the phone rings.
They don't move.

Leave it.

—I can't leave it. You know I can't leave it.

He pulls his hand away and answers the phone.

Yes? Hello?

307

(*brightly*) Morris. (It's Morris.) Yes. Sorry.

It's not, of course it's not late.

No, Morris, we were just, we were just, we were just . . .

—Here.

—We were just *here*. We were just enjoying the –

Well that's right: the evening, the beautiful evening. Did you see that sky, that fabulous sky?

Well yes, I *mean* earlier on. It *was* earlier on. It's dark now, of course it is – though quite starry, I should imagine.

Starry – as in bright – with stars.

Well I'll tell her, I'll certainly tell her, Morris. (He got the paint.)

You *didn't*?

Oh *really*? (*Chuckles.*)

(He found the other pot when he got back home.) So now you've got two, Morris.

I said: so / now you've got –

—Just tell him to go away.

—(What?)

—Tell him to leave us alone. Tell him to / go away.

—Well what an extraordinary place to find it. Listen, Morry . . . what if I were to call you back in the morning. Because the thing is, is we . . .

(*seriously*) Uh-huh, uh-huh, uh-huh.

Well how did that –

Uh-huh. Well how did that –

Uh-huh, uh-huh, uh-huh.

Well how did that *happen*? (Can you get me something to write with?)

Nothing, nothing, I just said how did it happen, Morris? When was this?

—What?

—Excuse me. (A pencil. Something to write with.) So
when exactly was this?

Corinne goes out.

Uh-huh, uh-huh.

Well hang on a minute, Morris, hang on a minute.
Because the fact is, is (a) I fully intended to make that
visit, and (b) regardless of any visit the man was
always going to die. This was a sick old man, Morris.
You've been there. You've seen that house. You've
seen him trying to breathe. You know his history. And
please don't let's forget that the man was a bastard.

Difficult? He was a manipulative old bastard,
Morris, as you well know.

*Corinne returns with a pencil. She also brings a
woman's bag – a handbag or miniature backpack.*

I take your point, I absolutely take your point.
Of course it doesn't look good, but that doesn't
necessarily mean it 'looks bad'. It doesn't necessarily
mean it *is* bad. Because it's simply a thing, Morris
(thank you), simply a thing, a thing that –
unfortunately – yes – happens.

Well yes, I did intend to visit. Obviously. The visit
was noted.

—Ask him / about the girl.

—The visit was noted. The intention to visit was noted.
(What?)

—Ask him about –

—Excuse me, Morris. (What?)

—Ask him about the girl. Tell him she's in pain.

Pause.

Well tell him.

—(Of course she's not in pain. She's asleep.) Morris? No. Nothing. Just a little / domestic –

—Then why does she take pain-killers? Why does she have / needles?

—Just a little domestic . . . (Please . . .) (*He gestures to be left alone.*) . . . Sorry. Yes. Of course I'm listening, Morry. It was just a little domestic (shit, fuck) no, nothing, I'm just getting myself tangled, Morris, in this flex. The phone here is something out of a *museum* . . . you have to rotate the . . .

That's right: the dial. Now listen, Morris, I'm assuming I have your support –

What? No no no, of course I don't, of course I don't feel 'accused'. (*Laughs.*) I know you just have to establish – which you are – which you have – the facts, the relevant facts. And then the two of us simply have to present –

Well of course I'm not expecting you to lie, Morris. No one has to lie. That wouldn't be appropriate. It's simply a matter of putting these events in some kind of order, some kind of intelligible order.

Okay, we'll talk again, let's talk again, Morris, in the morning.

Goodnight. (*He hangs up.*)

—What's happened?

—Nothing's happened. Where did you find that?

—Where did I find this?

—Where did you find that? Yes.

—I found it in your car. I found it under the seat. You obviously *did* pick it up. It didn't sound like you not to have picked it up, and there it was.

—Uh-huh.

—(*faint laugh*) Yes.

—You looked.

—Yes. Of course I looked. I looked / under the seat.

—You looked for the bag.

—Yes, I looked for the bag. I not only looked for the bag, I found the bag. Here is the bag.

She gently empties the contents of the bag onto the floor. Pause.

It's just that I suddenly feel, I suddenly feel – help me – I suddenly feel lost. I don't know who you are. I don't know what you want. Because I thought you'd stopped. I thought you were clean. But if you've stopped why are there needles in her bag? Whose needles are they? Are they yours? Did she *pay* you for these things? *How* did she pay you?

Pause.

Who is she? Have you any idea? You probably don't even know / her name.

—She got into the car, that's all.

—I see.

—She just got into the car.

—I see. She just got into the car.

—Exactly.

—And why was that?

—Why?

—Yes, why was that?

—To see a stone.

—To see a stone. She got into your car to see a stone.

—Yes.

—What stone?

—I've no idea what stone. Now put her things back into the bag. Don't touch her things. There's no reason to touch her things. She's asleep. Let her sleep. In the morning she'll wake up. And she'll leave.

Pause.

(*ending the story*) And this is what happened.

—What is what happened?

—This is. This is exactly all that happened. Don't look at / me like that.

—I thought you'd stopped. I thought you were clean. I thought that was the point of / *coming* here.

—Now put her things back please into the bag.

—Does Morris know?

—Of course he doesn't know.

—Get her out of here.

—How can I get her / out of here?

—Take her to Morris.

—Of course. Take her to Morris. 'Oh, good evening, Morris. I found this young woman unconscious on the track after shooting up in my Peugeot and I'd just like to get a second opinion.' 'Just the ticket, old boy. Wheel her into the library and sample a fine old malt while we discuss the imminent termination of your career and subsequent life of shame and / poverty.'

—What 'track'?

—What?

—What 'track'? What d'you mean, 'she got into the car'?

—Take her to Morris. Yes.

—What d'you mean, 'she got into the car'? When did she get into the car? Is that why Morris appeared?

—Why Morris appeared?

—Why he appeared. Why he asked where you were.

—Listen: I can't lie to you.

—You *have* lied to me. The *track*? You have already / lied to me.

—I'm trying to explain this.

—What track?

—I don't know. A track, a track, a track such as you find. *Such as one simply finds.* (*softly*) It was on the map. It was her idea. *She* got into the car. And I refuse to be blamed – not by you – not by Morris. All right, so I cancelled the visits, but the visits are of no importance. I know those people, they pick up the phone and it's doctor this doctor that just so I can give them a scrip for something they could buy themselves from Boots the fucking Chemists. Chest pains, chest pains. Well of

—Why did she get into your car? I thought you'd found her by the road but now she's getting into your car, you're driving along a track. She's complicit. Are you saying

313

she's complicit – or
what? – that you . . .
Listen to me. What exactly
are you saying, Richard?
Well? What *difference*?
What difference?

course he had chest
pains. The man was
eighty years old. What
difference could it possibly
make?

To bring this . . . person here while your children are
asleep. To have me look for this bag. To *worry* about
you. To crawl about in the dark under the car-seat
like an idiot while you're – what – washing off the
smell?

—Please.

—Washing off the smell, are you, and asking me what
difference it makes?

—Please: this is not helpful.

—Oh really? What is helpful, then? To pick up girls? To
entice them into your car? To drive them up / a *track*?
What?

The phone rings.

—Nobody was enticed. Don't speak like that. That's not
what this is about. Listen / to me.

—Then what *is* this about? Enlighten me. *Yes.*

Silence.
    The phone continues to ring on and on.
    Finally Richard answers it.

—Hello? (*brightly*) Morris.

Corinne leaves the room.

No no. I'm here. Definitely here.
    Uh-huh. Uh-huh. Oblivious. How long has it been
ringing, then? Because we were both completely obliv–

Not a problem, of course it's not a problem, only . . . only . . . I don't suppose there's any question of you doing this one, is there?

Corinne appears in the doorway, observing him.

Yup yup yup. Calm . . . Okay . . . Just calm down, Morris, and give me –

Yes. All right. Sorry. Give me the details.

Yup . . . yup . . . yup . . . got it. Tell them I'll be there in – what – twenty minutes.

Fifteen then. Fifteen. I will try my best to be there in fifteen minutes.

Well I do understand the urgency, Morry. Of course I understand the urgency. (*He hangs up.*)

He goes out, immediately returns with case, places it on table, pops open the lid, checks contents, snaps it shut.
   Pause.

—And if she wakes up?

Pause.

—What?

—And if she / wakes up?

—She's not going to wake up. Trust me.

He goes out rapidly.
   Corinne remains in the doorway.

(. . . stone)

III

Same scene, later.
Rebecca sits on a chair with a blanket over her
shoulders. Corinne watches her speak.

—The sun was shining. The trees were green, but each
green was different. I mean the green of each species
was a different green.

Pause.

And I'd found the stone. Yes. This . . . outpost . . . of
the empire. Only it wasn't just 'a stone' because it had
arms, like a chair. And I rested my arms along them.
I rested my arms along the arms of stone. And there
was a kind of congruence.

Pause.

—Oh really?

—Yes. A kind of congruence – what, does that surprise
you? – between the arms: the arms of stone, and the
arms of . . .

—Flesh.

—What?

—Flesh.

—Exactly. Between the arms of stone and – yes – exactly
– my arms of flesh. So – okay – I watched the trees.
I'm watching the trees. And each tree is green, but
each green is different. And in fact each *leaf* is
different. Each leaf within each tree is of a different

green. And they're all trembling. I mean each leaf is trembling, and the whole line isn't just bending, it's also waving. But ever so slightly. While the cold of the stone is – what – is seeping into me.

Pause.

Then it was getting dark.

—I thought it was light.

—It *was* light. Absolutely. It was very clear and light up there – so clear and light that you could see the dark coming.

Pause.

Then I woke up and this was over me.

—What was over you?

—This. This thing. This blanket was over me. I thought I had *died*. I thought, well okay, this is death.

Pause.

D'you have my watch?

—What?

—My watch. I was wearing a watch.

—Really?

—Yes. A gold watch.

—A gold watch.

—Yes. With a golden strap. A gold watch with a golden strap.

—It's on the table.

Rebecca goes to the table, letting the blanket fall. She slips on the watch, her back to Corinne.

—What is it you're looking at?

—I'm sorry?

—You're staring at me.

—We took the watch off. We thought you might damage it.

—Oh? We?

—My husband and I.

—My husband and I? (*faint laugh*)

—Where are you going?

—Can I get a glass of water through here?

—No. The other way.

—The other way.

—Yes. *That* way.

—The other way.

—Yes.

—*This* way?

Pause.

This way?

—Yes.

—Thank you.

—Through there.

—Well, thank you.

Rebecca goes out.

—You'll need to turn on the light.

—Is there a light? I don't see it. Yes – okay – I see it.

A light goes on, spilling faintly into the room. We hear Rebecca at the tap. Light goes out. She reappears in the doorway with a glass of water, sips it.

What happened to my bag? It spilled?

—Yes?

—How did it spill?

—Out.

—It spilled out.

—Yes. Yes, I'm afraid it did.

—(*amused*) What? Was there a *scene*?

—A scene?

—What did I do? Did I make a scene? My God, how / embarrassing.

—You didn't do anything. You were asleep. There wasn't a scene.

—But the bag . . .

—The bag spilled out.

Rebecca calmly gathers her things and puts them back in the bag, keeping out a pack of cigarettes.
    Corinne watches her.

He isn't here.

—Who isn't here?

—My husband. He isn't here.

—You mean you're alone?

—What? Yes. No. No. I mean he's out.

—Where?

—Why?

—What? (*Slight pause.*) Why what?

—Do you ask?

—Where he is?

—Yes.

—Why do I ask where Richard is?

—Yes. You know his name.

—His name is Richard.

—I know his name is Richard.

—Where is he then?

—He's out. He's covering.

—He's covering?

—He's covering, yes, for / his partner.

—D'you have an ashtray?

—What? No. We don't. Sorry.

—Then is there something I may use?

—Use?

—Use as an ashtray.

—What d'you mean? Like a dish?

—Yes, like a dish. Like a plate. Like a . . .

—What, like a cup? A coffee cup.

—A dish, a cup, a coffee cup – or just a plate, just an
ordinary / plate.

—No, I'm afraid there's nothing you can use as an ashtray. We don't have anything you can use / as an ashtray.

—No, you're right, it is disgusting. It is disgusting to wake in the night and to crave, my God yes, why do we immediately crave what will most do us harm? Coffee. A cigarette. Sex. (*faint laugh*) I'll just use the pack. I'll flick my ash right back into the pack.

She does so. Pause.

—Listen: there's something I have / to say to you.

—D'you mean Morris?

—I'm sorry?

—He's covering for Morris?

—Yes. Why? D'you know Morris?

—No, but I'd like to meet him. He sounds like a character.

—Oh yes, he's a character.

—You hate him?

—What?

—You hate Morris?

—(*faint laugh*) Is it / so obvious?

—Why do you hate Morris? *Completely* / obvious. Yes.

—Is it really that obvious?

—Well yes. You *hate* the man.

They both laugh.

Why do you hate Morris?

—You've never met him.

—No, but I'd like to. He reads Latin.

—What?

—Well doesn't he read Latin? Richard told me he / reads Latin.

—Yes, he reads Latin.

—Well then I'd like to meet him. I'd like to talk Latin with him. And history. I'd love to discuss history.

—You 'talk Latin' do you?

—Does that surprise you?

—No. Yes. Yes it does, actually. It does surprise me / very much.

—Oh really? Because I couldn't do what I do without Latin. I wouldn't *be* here without Latin.

—What *do* you do?

—What do I *do*? I study.

—You study.

—I study.

—You study Latin.

—I don't study Latin, no – I mean, yes, okay, I *study* it, but my *study*, what I study is History. And this is the place to be.

Pause.

If you're interested in History, then I guess this is the / place to be.

—I'm not interested in History.

—Everybody is interested in History.

—Perhaps where you come from. But I'm not. We're not. In fact, the opposite.

—The opposite?

—Yes.

—What opposite?

—That's not why we / came here.

—What opposite? Because the opposite of History is surely – forgive me – ignorance.

—That's not why we came here. We came here to live.

—To live.

—Yes. To live. Are you usually this / sententious?

—So you've not always lived in the country?

—What? No. Yes. *This* country? Yes.

—No. The country. Not *this* country. The country.

—The countryside.

—Yes. Okay. The countryside.

—No.

—Is that what you *call* it? The country*side*?

—No.

—Okay.

—It's the country. We call it the country.

—Okay. Good.

—*We* call it – I mean – the country, because we come from the town, but if you come from the country, then

you call it . . . I suppose you call it . . . (*Faint laugh.*)
I don't know what you call it.

—Home.

—Yes. Perhaps.

—You would call it home.

—Why would you call it home? Do you come from the
country?

—(*laughs*) Me? I come from the city. For me the city will
always be home. I say to people 'back home', whereas
for you . . .

—What?

—D'you say 'back home'?

—This is where we live. This is where our children will
live. This *is* our home.

—Exactly. Well exactly: you and your children have
nowhere to go / back to.

—This is our home. We don't want to 'go back'. We are
a family. We are here permanently.

—And is that – what? – because of an ideal? Permanently.
But how can you / be sure?

—What ideal? No. We just fell in love / with –

—You fell in love?

—Yes – with the house. I don't know what you / mean,
'ideal'.

—Well a rural – obviously – ideal. Virgil, for example,
his ideal of the country. Of the harmonious . . . of the
order of things, of the orderly cultivation of things. Of
the tasks appropriate to winter and spring, summer

and fall, the vines, the willow-beds, the. . . / almond
trees.

—We simply came here to change our lives a little, to . . .
and perhaps this sounds unreasonable – but yes, to be
happier, to aim at any rate / to be

—No, not at all.

—happier. To get away – yes – permanently – from the
city. It has nothing whatsoever to do / with Virgil.

—Not at all. To strive, you mean, to strive for your /
family's happiness.

—If you *can* get away. Assuming that it is because I think
that it is possible / to get away.

—The city makes people crazy.

—Yes.

—I've seen it. Crazy people. My *friends*.

—Yes.

—They don't sleep nights. They lie awake just listening,
just listening to the city.

—Yes.

—But they're terrified. They're terrified to leave.

—I know. Are they? Yes.

—In case they miss – yes they *are* – in case they miss the
opportunity, some opportunity which naturally may /
never come.

—But we did, you see. We did get away. And when he
showed me this house . . .

—I have some crazy friends. The stuff they do, the stuff
they crave, you would / not believe.

—He showed me the house – this house – and that convinced me.

—He convinced you. He convinced you to come.

—Yes.

—He convinced you that this was good.

—It is good. It is good. I didn't need / to be convinced.

—The land. The stream. The beautiful house.

—Yes. The beautiful house. Why not?

Pause.

What do you want from me?

—Your . . . husband – almost killed me tonight. Back there on the track. Or did he not mention that? (*Lights cigarette.*) Oh man, that was something. That was quite something. That was a *hit*.

Pause.

I thought I had *died*. Or did he not mention that?

—Okay, okay, okay. Yes. Listen to me.

—Before he 'went out'. Before he 'went to cover'. Before he left me here without an ashtray.

—Listen to me.

—What? What? Yes? Listen? Okay. (*Slight pause.*) Well okay: I'm listening / to you.

—You've woken up in a strange house. I understand that you're confused. It's a big house. It's the middle of the night. I don't know you. I don't know what you want. I *do* know – and listen to me – I do know that his primary concern has been for your safety. Is that clear to you?

326

My husband is a doctor. You are in a doctor's
house. You're an intelligent girl – a very – clearly –
intelligent girl – but I will not accept – neither of us
will accept – will not accept that you can simply
accuse him of – where are you going?

*Rebecca is getting up, putting her cigarettes back into
the bag.*

—I think I should leave. Intelligent girl? Fuck that. Fuck
that. Why did he bring me here? He must've been
totally out of it – out of his / fucking *mind*.

—You can't leave. No. There's nothing . . .

—Where is my / jacket?

—Please, there's nothing *out* there. There's no . . .

—I can't leave?

—. . . light. There's no . . . It's just *country*, there's no
light or . . .

—I can't leave your / house? *What?*

—Of course you can leave the house, but not now, not
while you're . . . Please be / sensible.

—Confused?

—Exactly.

—Because I'm not the one who is / confused.

—Not before we've talked.

—We have talked.

—Look: I just want to be honest with you, perfectly
honest with you.

—You want to be honest?

—Yes. I'm / trying to –

—Because the more you talk, the less you say.

—That's not true. I'm / trying to . . .

—The less you really say.

— . . . to explain. No.

—You're trying to be / *honest*?

—Alright, alright, alright.

Pause.

I'm asking you – which I realise I have perhaps no
right to ask you – I realise, I realise – but asking you
then to forget – appealing to you – may I? – to forget
this error (which I'm sure it was) of judgement.

You don't *know* him. He's not . . .

Yes, he's a man, obviously, but he's not . . .

And perhaps – I don't know – but perhaps you gave
him a sign, unwittingly gave him a sign which he
misread. Which is no excuse – of course not – no. But
maybe the sign – to him – d'you see? – who maybe
can't read these signs – *because he is a man* maybe
can't read these signs. Yes?

Pause.

His ignorance – yes – stupidity – yes, accepted. But to
do you harm, I will not believe. No. I can't. A girl – a
woman – a young woman accepts a ride from a man
she's never met. And perhaps for her it's . . . I don't
know what it is – it's a game? Is it a game? She's
young – she's not afraid – she gets into his car – on a
pretext – some pretext? – and however wrong this is –
however wrong *we* know this is – how does he (who
is after all human) interpret that?

He's wronged you – clearly wronged you – and
you're angry – as you have every right to be – but

328

then let *me* apologise. You will recover. For you it's just one afternoon, one night, from which you will soon recover. Whereas for us – and this is what I mean by honest – it's our life together – it's his whole position here – to speak quite frankly – that has been jeopardised.

Now if you need something – if you need . . . Because I don't know what you may want, what you may need – but if you need . . . / money, or –

—Just for an afternoon.

—What? Yes. I'm sorry if that / sounds blunt.

—(*quiet and intense*) But what d'you mean, 'just for an afternoon'? What d'you mean, 'a man she's never met'? Have you no inkling?

D'you really have no inkling?

And yet you condescend to me. You patronise me. With your house, your land, your children.

And accuse *me* of sententiousness?

Just for an afternoon?

He came to the country to *be with me*.

Yes.

Because of his longing to be with me.

Because of his greed to be with me.

'A man she's never met'? How can you *deceive* yourself? And then to *apologise* to me – on his behalf . . . (*faint laugh*) . . . in your own house?

Pause.

—I'd like you to leave.

—To touch my things – to take my things – to take / my *watch*.

—I said I'd like you to leave.

—The watch he gave me.

329

—Get out.

—But you wanted me to stay. I thought you wanted me to stay on account of my / confusion.

—I've changed my mind. I want you to leave. I want you to get out.

—Where can I go?

—I don't care where you go.

—Oh, shall I go to Morris?

Pause.

Shall I go to Morris? Shall I speak Latin? Shall I talk History?

(. . . paper)

IV

Same scene, later.
  Rebecca, alone.

—'This song of husbandry . . . of crops and beasts and
   fruit trees I was singing while great Caesar was
   thundering beside the deep Euphrates in war,
   victoriously for grateful peoples.' Grateful peoples.
   (*faint laugh*) But what did *he* know? About crops.
   Or trees. How did he know that the 'peoples' were
   grateful?

*Richard enters with a glass of water and gives it to
Rebecca.*

And how were the farms run? (Thank you.) I'll tell
you how the farms were run. By slaves. By the labour
of slaves. Which he neglects to mention.

—Please keep your voice down.

—But this is poetry. This is *pastoral*.

Pause.
  She sips.

—So you've not seen Corinne?

—What? Your wife? (*Slight pause.*) I've already told
   you: I woke up. I was alone. In a strange house. I was
   afraid. So no: I have not / 'seen Corinne'.

—You haven't heard her move about?

—I've heard no one move about. I've heard nothing.
   Why would your wife / move about?

—If she was awake. If she was awake, she would move about.

Pause.

She would pace about.

—Can I take a shower? Where is it?

—No.

—Is it through here?

—No. You can't. You can't – I'm sorry – take a shower.

—Do I go through here?

—No, that's . . . that's . . .

—*What* is it?

Pause.

What is it?

—You don't go through there.

— Where do I go?

—You don't. It makes a noise.

—What noise?

—Yes.

—Does it?

—Yes. I'm sorry.

Pause.

—I won't make a noise.

—You *will* make a noise. I'm sorry, but you *will* make a noise.

—What noise? I won't / make a noise.

—The noise it makes. The noise of . . .

—Your shower makes a noise? What / noise?

—The noise of showering.

—Of what?

—Of showering. The noise of / the water.

—Your shower makes a noise of showering?

—Unfortunately, yes.

Pause.

—You mean the water?

—The water and also the curtain makes a noise on its track.

—What kind of noise?

—A kind of screeching, a kind of / screeching noise.

—I won't touch – well in that case I simply won't touch the curtain.

—It makes a / noise. No.

—I'll just shower.

—No. I'm terribly sorry. No.

Pause.

You'll wake my wife. You'll wake / the children.

—How will I do that? I can't / take a shower?

—*Listen* to me.

—I mean how exactly do you propose to . . . propose to . . . enforce . . .

—What?

333

—Enforce – yes – this prohibition?

—Please, I'm just / asking you.

—With violence?

—I'm just asking you not to use / the shower.

—With violence? Really?

—No. Listen. Let me explain. The shower – not with violence – the shower is up the stairs . . .

—Okay.

—You go up the stairs, but the shower is through –

—Thank you. So I go up the stairs.

—Yes. But no – no, you don't go up the stairs because what I mean is, is you have to pass through their room. The shower is through the children's room. Now do you see?

—It's through your children's room.

—Yes.

—I see. Your children.

—Yes.

—But why is that?

Pause.

Why is your house designed like that? Why do you pass through your children's room to reach / your bathroom?

—It's not a house.

—It's not a house?

—No, it's not a house, it's a . . .

—What is it?

—I'm telling you what it is. You know what it is. You know it's not a house, it's a granary, it's a . . .

—It's a granary.

—It *was* a granary. It was for grain. It was not a house. *Now* it's a house. And of course I'm not – you know I'm not – threatening you. I'm appealing – simply – d'you understand – appealing to your reason.

—But is this reasonable?

—Is what reasonable?

—This . . . route.

—Route.

—This strange – yes – route to your bathroom. Is this a reasonable route?

—I believe so. Yes. In fact it's always been a very good route – an ideal, you could call it, route.

—Until now.

—*Even* now.

—But not for me.

—Not – that's right – for you. Come on.

—What?

—Come on. We're going.

—We're going? Where?

—I'm taking you back.

—I don't trust you to take me back.

—Of course you trust me.

335

—Why should I trust you?

—I'm taking you back.

—Why should I trust you? You left me.

—I left you, yes, but I didn't *leave* you, and now I'm taking you back. I've *come* back, and I'm *taking* / you back.

—But this is my home.

—This is not – I'm sorry – your home.

—Then why did you bring me here?

—You know why / I brought you here.

—Was it to offer me a position?

—To do what?

—To offer me a position? To help your wife? To be the maid. Was it to be the maid?

—She doesn't need help. She's very capable.

—Get a maid. Fuck the maid.

—I don't want to fuck the maid.

—Everyone wants to fuck the maid.

—Well not me. In fact the opposite.

—The opposite? Really? (*faint laugh*)

—Yes really. Is that / funny?

—And what is the opposite of fucking the maid?

—The opposite of fucking the maid is not fucking the maid.

They both laugh quietly. She takes his hand.

—So where have you been?

—It was a baby.

—Oh, was it sick?

—No, it was born.

—Did you hold it?

—Of course I held it.

—Did the mother hold it?

—Yes.

—Did it cry?

—It screamed. Why?

—Was it beautiful?

—They found it beautiful.

—The parents.

—Yes, the parents found it beautiful. And so did I.

Pause.

The father thanked me.

—He thanked you?

—He put his arm around me.

—He was grateful.

—He was very grateful. I'd delivered his son.

—It was a boy.

—It was a baby boy. Yes.

—It was a family.

—It had . . . become one. He wanted me to have a drink
with him . . .

337

—So you had a drink with him?

. . . but I wouldn't.

Pause.

—You should've had a drink with him. The man has become / a father.

—But I wouldn't. I . . . he . . . followed me down the stairs . . . and he . . . trapped me in the hall. It was a very small hall. The electricity meter was screwed to the wall, and I could see the disc, the silver disc of the meter going round and round. He said to me, 'Drink, doctor?' And I must've looked completely blank, because he said it again. The disc was spinning, and I was thinking, how can such a small house use so much electricity? There must be something on – a fire – a freezer – drawing the current. 'I'm having one,' he said, 'what about you?' And he had a big . . . name on his shirt. The name of a brand. The name of the brand of shirt . . . *on* his shirt. He was so happy. He was so hopeful.

Pause.

—Well of course he was happy. You had delivered his son.

—But I said, 'No. I have to go. I have to work.'

—You disappointed him. He wanted to celebrate.

—No. That's just the thing. He looked relieved.

She grips his hand more tightly.

Don't hurt me.

—I'm not hurting you.

—I said: don't hurt me.

338

—What? Does that hurt?

—Yes. It hurts. Stop it. What is it?

—Really? Does that hurt?

—Yes.

He pulls his hand out of her grip. The tiny scissors drop to the floor.

You've cut my hand.

—I've what?

—You've made a hole in my hand.

—A hole in your hand?

—Yes.

—Oh my – you're angry.

—Yes.

—(*laughing*) You're so angry, Richard.

—Keep your voice down.

—I've made a hole in your hand? Is it deep? Are you in pain?

Pause.

Squeeze it.

—I'm squeezing it.

—Let me squeeze it.

—Don't touch me.

He allows her to take his hand.

—It's only the flesh.

—There *is* only flesh.

She sucks the wound, releases his hand.
  He looks at her, smiles.

—What?

—There's blood on you.

—Where?

—Here on your face.

He touches her by the mouth.
  She lets his fingers rest there a moment, then breaks away, and wipes her mouth on her sleeve.

—Can I see them?

—See what?

—Your kids?

—No. I've said.

—You've said?

—Yes, I've said.

—You've spoken.

—That's right.

Pause.

—What're their names?

—They don't have names.

—They don't have names.

—No.

Pause.

You know they don't have names. We have an agreement.

—I don't think we have an agreement any more.

—We have an agreement. Nothing's changed.

—Everything has changed. 'Nothing has changed'?
What?

—They don't have names.

—For one thing, I'm *here*.

—No. You're wrong. You're not here.

—I'm not here?

—No.

—So where am I?

Pause.

I promise to tip-toe. Let me just tip-toe up and see.
Let me just listen to them breathe. Or, if they're
awake, I could tell them a story.

—They don't want to hear a story.

—But everybody wants to hear a story, don't they?
I could say: Hello. I'm Rebecca. I'm the maid. Let me
tell you a story. Would you like me to tell you a story?

—They don't want / to hear a story.

—Oh yes please, Rebecca, tell us a story. Well once upon
a time, children, there was a girl, there was a bright
young girl, and she was sick, and she needed some
medicine. So she went to a doctor –

—Listen to me.

—She went to a doctor and she said, doctor, doctor, it
hurts, I need some medicine. But the doctor wouldn't
give her any. He said, go away – don't waste my time –

341

I have no medicine. So she went back again and she said, doctor, doctor, it really hurts, I need some medicine. And this time the doctor went to the door. He locked the door. He said: I need to take a history – roll up your sleeve. So she rolled up her sleeve and the doctor took a history. Then, children, he got one instrument to look into her eyes. And another instrument to listen to her heart. And when he'd looked into her eyes and listened to her heart, he asked her to undress.

—Rebecca.

—He asked her to undress. And when she'd undressed, he said: I see now how very sick you are – you need some medicine. She said: Doctor, am I going to die? He said: No, it's simply that your eyes are very dark and your skin is very pale. Your skin is so thin that when I touch it like this with my lips I can feel the blood moving underneath. You're sick, that's all. You need some medicine. So the treatment began.

The treatment was wild, children. It could take place at any time of day or night. In any part of the city. In any part of her body. Her body . . . became the city. The doctor learned how to unfold her – like a map.

Until one day the bright young girl decided the treatment would have to end – because the more medicine she took, the more medicine she craved – and besides, she was leaving for the country.

Now this made the doctor very angry. Because he'd broken all the rules – as he saw it – for her. Not just the kind of rules you children have – take off your shoes, wash your hands – but grown-up rules. Laws. He'd broken all these rules – these laws – and he was very angry. In fact he wept. You bitch, he said. You little bitch.

342

Because you see there'd been a terrible
misunderstanding. Since the thing the bright young
girl bitch called treatment, the doctor – who of course
was sick himself – who craved medicine himself –
imagined to be – what? – something personal.
Something human. Which is why / he followed her.

—Listen, listen, listen. Rebecca. What / we need to –

—He followed her. He brought his / *family*.

—What we / need to –

—Okay. Good. Yes. Tell me what / we need.

—Because there is a limit – not what we need – but
don't you see there is a limit to what we . . .

—A limit?

—. . . to what we can – a limit, yes – usefully – tonight –
don't you see – to what we can . . .

—Hope. Hope to achieve.

—Yes. No. No. To what we can . . . to what the two of
us can . . . / *say*.

—Achieve in words.

—Yes, to what we can – exactly – achieve / in words.

—You see, I don't believe that. I think that is so totally /
dishonest.

—I mean tonight, tonight when the two of us are . . .

—*I'm* not tired.

—. . . when we are – exactly – tired – so tired that we /
can't think.

—Because I refuse to believe that. There's not a limit to
what can be said, only a limit to how honest we are
prepared to be. *I'm* not tired. I / can think.

343

—Well I am. You've been sleeping. I've been working. I've / been driving.

—So tell me what it is you think / we can't say.

—I've been working. I'm not prepared to have / this conversation.

—Not prepared? Just tell me.

—Tell you what?

—Just tell me what it is you think we can't say.

—How can I tell you what I can't – I *beg* your pardon? – say? *What?*

—Exactly. Well exactly. Because there is / *no such thing.*

—(*softly*) I should've left you on the fucking track.

—What?

—I should've left you on the fucking track.

—Left me?

—And that is the truth. *Left* you there.

—You mean for dead?

—I mean – yes I do – for dead.

Pause.
Rebecca begins to laugh.

—You know she thought I had given you a sign? (*Slight pause.*) Your wife. She thought I had given you 'a sign'. She wanted to apologise for you. Isn't that cool? (*Slight pause.*) She's actually quite attractive. Why did you always say how unattractive she was? How you had to turn the light out? (*Slight pause.*) You / lied to me.

344

—You've talked to her.

—You lied to me. What? Yes. Well yes, certainly I talked
to her. (*Slight pause.*) Oh, don't worry. She's gone.
Some while ago. She took the kids, and left. (*Slight
pause.*) They were so sleepy. And the way she bundled
them. My God, the way she bundled them out.

Pause.
  They don't move.

Don't hurt me.

—I'm not hurting you.

Pause.
  He looks at her.

—Then don't look at me.

—I'm not looking at you.

—Then don't look at me.

They stare at each other.

(. . . scissors)

V

Two months later.

Sunday morning. The same space, but transformed by daylight.

A huge window looks out onto the countryside.

Corinne is opening envelopes. She takes out the cards, reads them, lays them down in a pile.

Richard enters with a glass of water as she opens the last card – his – which is why she turns and says:

—Thank you.

—D'you like it?

—D'you *mean* this?

—Do I . . . what? . . . mean? Sorry?

—(*laughing*) This. *This.*

—Well look, I'm a doctor, I'm not a . . . I don't pretend to be a . . . / *writer.*

—What you've written. But what you've written here – d'you mean this?

—Yes. Well yes I do. Of course I mean what / I've written.

—Thank you.

—What?

—*Thank* you.

—It's a promise.

—Will you keep it?

—What?

—I said will you / keep it?

—I am keeping it. You *know* I'm keeping it.

—Keeping yourself clean.

—Keeping myself – yes – extremely clean.

Both smile. She takes the water from him. Pause. Then she takes a sip.

How is the water?

—How is the water?

—Yes.

—Delicious. Cold. Why?

—What does it taste of?

—Taste of? Nothing.

—Really?

—Why? What should it / taste of?

—You used to think it had a taste. When we first came here. It worried you.

—(*laughs*) What did?

—(*laughs*) The taste of the water. The taste of the water worried you.

—The taste of the water worried me? What did it taste of?

—It didn't taste of anything.

—Then why did it worry me? It doesn't worry me now.

—Good.

—Well does it you?

—It never did worry me. Can I get you some more?

—What?

—Can I get you some more / water?

—I've still got this to drink.

She drinks the rest of the water. He takes the glass.
She begins to laugh.

—What? What is it? What?

—It's just that you're being so . . .

—Am I? What?

—So . . . solicitous.

—Really?

—Yes.

—Solicitous.

—Yes.

—What does that mean?

—Don't you know what / it means?

—Well tell me then what it means. No, I don't. I've / no idea.

—To care. It means to care.

—Okay.

—Don't you believe me?

Slight pause. They both laugh.

Why are you looking at me like that? Don't you /
believe me?

—No, it's just that I have in my mind, why do I have in
my mind, because I have in my mind that it's about
sex.

—Sex? No. Nothing to do / with sex.

—Paying in fact for sex.

—It means to care – to be caring. That is 'solicit'. You
mean solicit – to . . . / solicit someone.

—You mean like a solicitor.

—No, I don't mean like a solicitor.

They both laugh.

—But it's not wrong is it?

—What? To pay for sex?

—To care. It's not wrong of me to care.

—About what?

—About you.

—I don't know.

—You don't know? You mean it's wrong?

—I don't know.

Pause. She fiddles with the cards, looks up, smiles.

No – of / course not.

—You should put up your cards.

—What? I don't want to.

—Yes. Stand them up. Stand them all up. Put them /
in a row.

—I don't want to. It will make me feel old.

—But you're not old.

—(*faint laugh*) Why d'you keep looking at me / like that?

—Old? You're not old. And I'm looking at you – if I am indeed 'looking at you' – precisely because you're not old. You look – you still look like a girl.

—(*laughs*) What 'girl'?

—(*laughs*) *Like* a girl. Not *what* girl. Like / a girl.

—(*laughs*) I don't want to look like a girl. What if I don't want to look like a girl? Where are you going?

—To get something.

—I don't want any more water.

—That's not what I'm getting.

—What are you getting then?

—(*humorously*) Ah-*ha*.

He goes out, taking the empty glass. She looks through the cards.

—D'you know what I was thinking – because I was opening these and I was thinking I'd like someone to've died and there to be a big cheque.

—(*off*) What?

—A cheque. A big cheque.

—(*off*) Who do you know who could've died?

—Anyone I know could die. People do die. My parents. My parents are a perfect example of people who / could die.

—(*off*) Your parents – I'm terribly sorry – but your parents are not / going to die.

—I would like my parents to have collided with the side of a mountain in South America and there to be no survivors. That way it would be painless and they would stop sending me cards with puppies on them / every year.

—(*off*) You can't say that.

—I can't say puppies? What are you doing / in there?

—(*off*) You can't say that about / your parents.

—I can say what I like about / my parents.

—(*off*) You have money. You don't need money. You live in a big house / in the country . . .

—Not real money. Not the kind of money some / people have.

—(*off*) . . . and your parents have nothing. If they *were* to die – and I'm sure it would be in agony –

—(*laughs*) Don't.

—(*off*) Yes. The utmost – knowing them – (*He reappears, holding a parcel.*) – deliberate agony. Then you would receive nothing.

—I'd probably get a bill.

—You would in fact – yes – get a bill.

—A big bill.

—You'd be left with nothing.

—Less than nothing.

—Just the memory of their agony.

—Don't.

—You'd be left with the memory of their agony and a bill for repatriating their remains. From wherever.

—I know.

—From Chile.

—Don't.

—Or Peru.

—(*smiles*) What's this?

—It's for you. It's a present.

—I don't need a present.

—Of course you need a present. Open it.

—What is it?

—Open it.

> *Pause. She starts to unwrap it.*
> *Inside the wrapping paper is a cardboard box.*
> *Inside the box is a pair of shoes.*
> *The shoes appear quite sober and elegant, but at the same time there is something unsettling about them – and this may not be apparent until Corinne puts them on. Perhaps, for example, they are a little too high for her.*

—Thank you.

—D'you like them?

—They look very expensive.

—They are very expensive. Put them on.

> *She puts them on.*

—How did you know my size?

—I don't know your size. I took a shoe.

—You took a shoe?

—I took a shoe – yes – to the shoe shop.

She stands up.

—Like the Prince.

—What?

—Like / the Prince.

—That's right. In a fairy tale. How do they feel?

—I don't know.

—Aren't they comfortable?

—They're very comfortable.

—Then what do you mean?

—I'd need to walk in them.

—Well walk in them then.

She walks. She turns. She smiles.

—So?

—You look . . . transformed.

—(*laughs*) Transformed? Into what?

—Don't you like them?

—It's strange.

—What is?

—To be given things.

—It's normal to be given things.

—Yes.

—It's perfectly normal, Corinne, to be given things.

—Yes. Is it?

—Well of course it is. You know it is. They suit you.

—Do they?

—Very much. You look quite different.

—Is that what you want?

—What? Yes. No. I just want you to be happy.

—Well I am happy.

—That's all I want.

—Well I am happy.

Slight pause. She walks again in the shoes, turns and smiles.

—I can take them back. I can change them. *You* can change them. We can go together and / change them.

—Don't do that. Why do that?

Phone.

—You don't like them.

—I love them. Really. Thank you. (*She picks up phone.*) Hello?

Sophie. Hi. Good morning. How are they? Did they sleep?

(*laughs*) Really? Really? Well that's marvellous.

No, it's a treat, it's a real birthday treat. You've been so –

No, you've been really kind to us.

Well . . . Richard made me breakfast . . . Yes, and then I opened my cards . . . Yes, and then I opened my present.

Shoes. He's given me a pair of shoes.

Yes. Lovely. I'm wearing them now. Apparently I look transformed.

I don't know. They make me feel rather . . .

—(*kissing the back of her neck*) Decadent.

—(What?)

—Decadent. They make you feel / decadent.

—(*laughs*) He's telling me I'm decadent. (Stop. I'm talking to Sophie.)

—Deeply decadent.

—Nothing. Sorry. He's just being a little . . . (You're distracting me. Stop.) He's just being a little . . . stopping me from / talking.

—(*moving away*) Ask her, did she find the money?

—Very typical, I'm afraid. (What?) Excuse me, Sophie. (What?)

—Did she find the money?

—(What money?) Hello? Yes. Nothing, it's just / Richard, he –

—The money I put in the cup.

—He's asking me if you found the money he put / in the cup.

—I put some money – that's all – in the cup.

—(She says you shouldn't have.) Well of *course* you should be paid.

—I just wondered if she's / found it.

—A mistake? What kind of mistake?

As Sophie explains, Corinne bends over and slips off the shoes.

Uh-huh . . . uh-huh . . . Really? Well if that's what he gave you, then I assume that's what he meant / to give you.

—I felt generous. I thought she might like to go out and / buy something.

—(*laughs*) I'm sure he didn't mean to *frighten* you – he was just being generous.

—Frighten her? Of course I didn't mean to / frighten her.

—Of *course* you should keep it. You're *meant* to keep it.

—She has to keep it.

—You have to keep it, Sophie. Now listen: do tell them that Mummy –
   That's right: tell them that Mummy and Daddy are . . .

—Coming to get them after tea.

—Are . . . missing them very much and coming to get them after tea.
   Okay.
   Thanks, Sophie. (*Hangs up.*) Why did you give her so much money? She said she was terrified.

—By what?

—By all that money.

—By me?

—No. By all that money. Not by you. She likes you.

—How can you tell?

—You can just tell. Her voice changes.

—What d'you mean: she likes me?

—I just mean she likes you. Her voice changes when she uses / your name.

—You mean I flirt with her?

—I mean she flirts with *us*. Takes our children. Scrubs our floors. Asks for nothing.

—That's because she despises us. It's because she despises you and me and everything we stand for.

—Well she has a very strange way of showing it and I don't think we 'stand' for anything. People don't 'stand' for things, they . . .

—People don't stand for / things.

— . . . exist.

—What?

—They exist, they simply exist. Perhaps what you mean to say is that you despise your*self*.

—(*laughs*) Why should I despise myself?

—(*laughs*) Well *I* don't know. I don't know why you should despise yourself. Okay, she's poor, but she has a cottage, she has a . . .

—Telephone.

—A telephone, a cooker . . . So why do I have to feel something? Please don't ask me to / *feel* something.

—I'm not asking you to feel anything.

—Because I don't. I can't.

Silence.

—You know what I was thinking: I was thinking that perhaps we could change the . . .

—Change the what?

—The design – the design, actually, of the house. I've been thinking about upstairs, particularly / about upstairs.

—What's wrong with upstairs? I like upstairs. I like this house. I don't want / to change it.

—I'm not saying I don't like the house, I'm just saying perhaps we could change one or two things.

—Upstairs.

—Yes. Well yes – because the way it's arranged / isn't logical.

—Whose idea is that?

—Sorry?

—Why isn't it logical? Why should it be / logical?

—Whose *idea*? No one's. Mine. My idea.

—Morris's? Is it Morris's idea?

—To change the house? Morris?

—(*laughs*) Yes. Given his / thirst for control.

—(*laughs*) Of course not. *What* did you say?

—(*laughs*) His thirst – yes – for control.

—His thirst.

—Yes. Well surely you've noticed. Don't tell me that after all this time you still haven't noticed his thirst / for control.

—His thirst for control? Listen, I'm just talking about changing one or two things upstairs, that's all. The layout upstairs. Which is nothing whatsoever to do

I can assure you with Morris. Morris has been very good to us.

—Of course.

—To both of us.

—Yes. He lied.

—He defended my judgement. He did not / lie.

—Exactly. He lied. You left a man to die and Morris lied for you.

Pause. Corinne begins to laugh.

—(*smiles*) What?

—Oh God, I thought you'd lost your sense of humour. I thought, oh no, he's finally lost his famous sense of humour.

—But in fact you were wrong.

—In fact I was wrong.

—In fact my famous sense of humour survives intact.

—In fact your famous sense of humour does – remarkably – survive / intact.

—So. Listen. What shall we do? Shall we go out?

—What?

—Go out. Let's drive somewhere. Let's get out the map.

—Okay.

—We could visit the Wall. We could have a picnic.

—Okay.

—Because we live in the country and we never . . .

—I know.

—We never . . .

—Exactly. You're right.

—. . . experience . . .

—It's true . . .

—. . . experience those things.

—The Wall.

—The Wall. The Fell.

—You mean walk along the Wall.

—Walk along the Wall. Walk the Fell. Why have we never walked along / the Wall?

—Have we really never walked along the Wall?

—Never.

—I could wear my shoes, then.

—What?

—I could wear my shoes.

—I don't think so.

—Oh, don't you think so?

—It's wet.

—Is it?

—It rained.

—Did it?

Pause.

—Is something wrong?

—No, nothing's wrong.

—Let's go out then.

—I've *been* out.

—I don't think so.

—I think I have.

—When was that?

—Yesterday evening. I went on a trip.

—What trip?

—You took the children to Sophie's, and I went on a trip, that's all.

—You didn't tell me.

—Oh, didn't / I tell you?

—What trip?

   Pause.

   What trip?

—Why?

—I'd like to know.

—You'd like to know what I did with my evening.

—Well yes – yes, I would like to know what you did with your / evening.

—You'd gone. I locked up. I crossed the yard. I got into my car. I twisted the mirror. I looked at myself.

   Pause.

—How did you look?

—Complicit.

—Show me.

361

—(*smiles*) What?

—Show me how you looked.

—I looked complicit.

—Show me.

She looks down – seems about to try – but then laughs.

—I can't.

—Can't you do it?

—Not if I don't feel it.

—Oh, don't you feel it?

—No. Complicit? No. Why / should I?

—But why did you twist the mirror? Tell me.

—Oh, to reverse. I needed to reverse – or no – not needed – but I did – reverse. Reversing gave me enormous pleasure. Watching the house as it shrank gave me the most enormous pleasure. It got so small so quickly. I'd backed out on to the road before I knew it, and the house smiled back at me through the trees.

Pause.

—So *you* were smiling.

—Well yes – I must've been. (*She smiles.*) Probably because the evening was so perfect. So light.

—You mean the sun was nowhere near setting.

—The sun – that's right – was nowhere near setting and the moon was up. It was flecked – this will amuse you – like an egg.

—What kind of egg?

—Like a grey egg.

—What kind of egg?

—Well, a bird's egg, / obviously.

—So then you began to drive.

—What?

—So then you began / to drive.

—So then I began – yes, obviously – to drive away from the house. I turned right at the fingerpost and the road was so utterly long and straight I knew it must be old. I knew it must be nothing to do with me, this road, this old road. I didn't really like it being old. I didn't really like it being straight. Because after all I'd gone for an aimless drive and now – well – you can imagine – this road was coercing me. So when it ran out, I was pleased. It stopped at a ditch. No sign – just a ditch.

Pause.

—So that was the end of your little trip. That's what you did with your evening. Drove to a ditch.

—What? No. I got out of the car – oh no, my trip was just beginning – I got out of the car and I leapt across the ditch.

—(*laughs*) You leapt across the ditch.

—(*laughs*) Yes. Like a mad thing. And I began to run up the hill. You should've seen me running up that hill. I thought: I haven't run like this for no reason since I was a girl. Everything flapped – my hair . . . my clothes . . .

—You weren't dressed for the country.

—No. I had utterly failed to dress for the country.

363

My dress was flapping round my legs like a flag
and I knew I should go back to the car but I knew
I wouldn't go back to the car.

—Why wouldn't you go back to the car?

—BECAUSE I DIDN'T WANT TO GO BACK TO THE
CAR. (*quietly*) I didn't want to go back to the car, not
now I had discovered the track.

It wasn't at all what I'd imagined, not the hard thin
sheep or goat track I'd imagined. No, it was . . .
broad, and littered with shale. At least, I think it was
shale. It made a noise as I walked, a kind of clatter.
And that's when I realised, as I slithered and clattered
my way along the shale, that there was nothing
human.

Well *I* was there, obviously. *I* was human, but
nothing else was. I looked out for human things.
Because I thought I might see – you know – a piece
of wire or a spent cartridge with the top blown out.
I thought I might see a plastic bag snagged in a hedge.
Only there was no hedge. I thought I might see a
needle or a piece of brick. I longed – you know – to
see something human like a needle, or a piece of brick
mixed with the shale. Or to hear – even to hear
something human other than myself. Other than my
feet. Other than my heart. A plane. Or children
screaming. Only there was nothing. Not even a track
now. Because the track – just like the road – stopped.
Or it . . . what did it do? . . . it 'gave out'.

The track – that's right – gave out, and now there
were just . . . clumps. Which meant, of course,
stepping – although I needn't – but stepping from one
clump to the next. You should've seen me stepping the
way a child steps from one clump to the next until I
reached the stone. Well I say 'the stone', but the stone
had arms, like a chair. So you could sit . . . within the

stone. You could rest your arms along the arms of the stone, and from within the stone, look out at the land.

Pause.

— And how was the land?

— Oh, the land was lovely. But the stone was cold. I don't think the sun had ever warmed it. I was afraid it would stick to my skin, like ice. And then Morris appeared.

— Morris? What did he want?

— Well that's what I said. I said, 'What is it, Morris? What do you want?' He said, 'I've been following you for hours. Didn't you hear me calling you? You dropped this.'

— Dropped what?

— Well that's what I said. I said, 'Dropped what, Morris? Just what have I dropped?' 'Your watch, of course,' he said. And he dangled it in front of my face from its golden strap, so I could see all its tiny works. I said, 'I'm afraid you're mistaken. It's very beautiful, but it's not mine. It's very delicate, but it isn't mine.' Which is when I noticed — and this will amuse you — that the stone had started to devour my heart.

Pause.

— Oh really?

— The stone had started to devour my heart. Yes. Why? Does that surprise you? I said to Morris, 'Morris. Help me. This stone is devouring my heart.' Only I didn't say it like that, softly like that. I said it like a mad thing. Which is why, I suspect, he gripped my shoulders to establish a certain authority. And when he'd established a certain authority, he said, 'It's only a stone. There's no need to shriek. How could a stone do that?' I said, 'I don't know, Morry, I thought perhaps you would be able to tell me.' He said, 'Are you afraid?' I said, 'Well yes, Morry, of course I'm afraid. I don't seem able to move and this stone is devouring my heart. When I get up from this stone, what if my heart has gone? What if I have to spend the rest of my life simulating love?'

The phone rings.

And Morris said, 'I'm sure you simulate love very well. I'm sure the two of you will simulate love immaculately.' (*faint laugh*) He's a character.

—Am I not, then?

—Not what?

—Am I not a character?

—Oh yes – you're a character – very definitely a character – but quite a different character. Kiss me.

The phone continues to ring.

—I have kissed you.

Pause.

—I have kissed you.

—Then kiss me again.

Neither moves. The phone continues to ring.

(. . . stone)